WHY

HOPE?

THE STAND
AGAINST
CIVILIZATION

JOHN ZERZAN
INTRODUCTION BY LANG GORE

Why Hope?
The Stand Against Civilization
Published in 2015

A Feral House book
ISBN 978-1-62731-019-2

Feral House
1240 W. Sims Way Suite 124
Port Townsend WA 98368
www.FeralHouse.com
Book design by D. Collins

10 9 8 7 6 5 4 3 2 1

TABLE OF CONTENTS

INTRODUCTION

The Absent Age
THINKING ABOUT AN UNTHINKABLE REBELLION

I n 1846 Søren Kierkegaard essentially anticipated the salient feature of the postmodern age—where reality is always screened
and the defining activities are Sitting and Watching—in an essay
titled *The Present Age*. He noted:

> A revolutionary age is an age of action; ours is the age of adver-
> tisement and publicity. Nothing ever happens but there is imme-
> diate publicity everywhere. In the present age a rebellion is, of all
> things, the most unthinkable.

*How much more unthinkable must rebellion be in an absent age,
where "all that once was directly lived has become mere representation"*
(Debord). Where domination assumes "a labyrinthine form without a
centre," to borrow the description of Gothic novel *Melmoth the Wanderer*, must any prospect of revolt be absent as well?

If so, our humiliation is complete. Michael Bakunin's keenest insight
was this:

> *"Three elements or, if you like, three fundamental principles constitute the
> essential conditions of all human development, collective or individual, in
> history: (1) human animality; (2) thought; and (3) rebellion."*

Some of us know we are animals, all of us imagine we think, many
of us would like to be in revolt. Yet who can abide the endless publicity
surrounding revolt? And who can abide the endless, alas!, deference to
Karl Marx, who more than anyone has dominated the publicity surrounding revolt?

Someone has said that history is made by those with a sense of style. Marx emerged from the First International ascendant over Bakunin thanks in part to the profound influence Shakespeare had on his style. In his *Economic and Philosophical Manuscripts* he quotes *Timon of Athens,* Act IV, Scene 3, and remarks:

"Shakespeare brings out two properties of money in particular: (1) It is the visible divinity, the transformation of all human and natural qualities into their opposites, the universal confusion and inversion of things; it brings together impossibilities; (2) It is the universal whore, the universal pimp of men and peoples."

Shakespeare indeed offers a key to anyone wishing to understand "the universal confusion and inversion of things." No matter what any line of Shakespeare may be about, it is at the same time almost always about something else. Marx recognized the utility of such a style in confronting a world that seems to be one thing, but almost always is something else.

Everyone knows Marx seemed to be about revolution, but wound up being all about something else, right? Roberto Calasso put it succinctly in *The Ruin of Kasch:*

"Marx is a prisoner of the Enemy he attacks; his adversary's body falls on him and smothers him. Marx has the definitive vision of the machine for demolishing limits, which he calls capitalism, yet he questions not the limit but the machine. He wants to design a better machine, which will demolish limits without ever jamming, without crises. Like a great mechanic, he has a loving, passionate knowledge of the capitalist machine. Concerning the limit, he shares that machine's illusions. What offended him was not so much and not only the iniquity which capital engendered, but the fact that capital was preparing to become an obstacle to production, an antiquated and sclerotic form compared with the immensity of what was possible. Nobody has ever dreamed the dream of capital with as much faith as Marx was able to muster in his spirit. He was like a young man from the provinces who takes seriously, with despairing gravity, the customs of the metropolis—that is how Marx viewed capital."

The sophistication with which Marx depicts the infinite fluidity of capital has obscured, however, a very unsophisticated truth: capital is plunder, and not only engenders iniquity, but was indeed engendered by iniquity.

The resources extracted from the worlds forced open by Europeans in the fifteenth and sixteenth centuries were of such astonishing volume that feudal society exploded from within. That made possible the more clever and dynamic system of extraction and exploitation which obtains currently.

Clever, because it emphasizes how different the industrial world of today is from the agricultural world of yesterday, not to mention the gatherer-hunter world of the years before yesterday. The good conscience of capital is that the Conquest was not carried out by capitalists. But the bad conscience of civilization is that the men who carried out the Conquest were civilized.

Just like many today, they believed in patriarchy, property, and authority. And like other civilized Europeans before them such as the Greeks and Romans, they believed in chattel slavery; their successors used it for centuries to eventually create societies so fabulously wealthy they now find workers as well as slaves superfluous. *Mohawk Nation News recently estimated around 80% of the world's population has been rendered redundant by the global commodity production system.*

In a world where we are all on the margins, John Zerzan has nothing but contempt for anything but a marginal life.

For several decades now, John has been at the cutting edge of contestation with authority. He undermines our conditioning by identifying it merely as the replication of domestication—thereby making it more hateful. He relentlessly unravels all the strands woven together so cunningly to contain any attempt to break out of lines laid down well before capitalists came along.

The present collection of essays continues the overarching thrust of John's scholarship, unveiling the post-apocalyptic nature of our times by noting the apocalypse was yesterday, several thousand years ago, to be precise, and that nothing produced by civilization can ever redeem the systematic attempt it has undertaken these (very) few millennia to destroy or alienate any human connection with the Earth.

In fact, when civilized Europeans imposed themselves everywhere on Earth, they created a terminal crisis for themselves by their very contact with indigenous societies.

Suddenly, those with eyes to see and ears to hear could recognize that patriarchy, property and authority, and certainly slavery, were neither necessary nor desirable, let alone determined by "human nature." Early New England colonist Cotton Mather worried that the proximity of gatherers and hunters would prove fatally alluring to many in the new colonies, given the evident ease and richness of their life compared to the constant toil required of farmers, let alone servants.

The crisis continues—the allure (for better or worse) has only deepened with the developments of recent decades, all of which establish unmistakably that the true nature of civilization is regress, not progress. As a character says in Christopher Isherwood's *Frankenstein: The True Story*, "The process is reversing itself." All that ever changes, really, is the rate of acceleration of the reversion, always and ever faster, as John reminds us in the essay included here titled "Faster."

So what else is new? This was clearly recognized in the so-called East by the Taoists, who saw domestication as debasement, most tellingly in Chuang Tzu's chapter titled "Horses' Hooves":

"The potter said, 'I know how to use clay, how to mold it into rounds like the compass and into squares as though I had used a T-square.' The carpenter said, 'I know how to use wood: to make it bend, I use the template; to make it straight, I use the plumb line.' However, is it really the innate nature of clay and wood to be molded by compass and T-square, template and plumb line? It is true, nevertheless, that generation after generation has said, 'Po Lo [the first horse breaker] is good at controlling horses, and indeed the potter and carpenter are good with clay and wood.' And the same nonsense is spouted by those who rule the world."

Thomas Merton's translation of another chapter's title from the same book makes a parallel point all by itself: "When Life Was Full There Was No History."

A similar attitude among Cynics emerged in the so-called West about the same time: "Consider the beasts yonder and the birds, how much freer from trouble they live than men, and they are, and how each of them lives the longest life possible, although they have neither hands nor human intelligence. And yet, to counter-balance these and their other limitations, they have one very great blessing—they own no property," as Dio Chrysostom put it, in words evoking and also transcending the well-known phrases of the Sermon on the Mount.

Thinking about rebellion leads invariably to considerations of method. How John does what he does—surveying the endless emptiness of "a labyrinthine form without a centre"—deserves a brief discussion.

In *The Present Age* Kierkegaard noted: "From now on the great man, the leader (according to his position) will be without authority because he will have . . . understood the diabolical principle of the leveling process; he will be *unrecognizable; he will keep his distinction hidden like a plain-clothes policeman, and his support will only be negative, i.e., repelling people, whereas the infinite indifference of abstraction judges every individual and examines him in his isolation.*" This order is dialectically the very opposite of that of the Prophets and Judges, and just as the danger for them lay in their authority not being recognized so nowadays the unrecognizable is in danger of being recognized, and of being persuaded to accept recognition and importance as an authority, which could only hinder the highest development.

An important contribution to John's "unrecognizability" is his choice of weapon. The bibliographic essay is perfect for preserving a quality of indigestibility, as it resists betraying a sense of style. Yet its style is apt indeed if one desires to undermine any accretion of authorial authority. It seems to defer endlessly to others, citing always an outside source for whatever is asserted.

Yet this is precisely, if only partly, why John speaks with authority, unlike the attorneys and academics. If it's magic, one might say about John's essays, as the late Roberto Bolano said about Castellanos Moya's books, the magic is in the "will to style." It's both paradoxical and perfectly appropriate that John's writings should have such authority given the unassuming quality of his personal style.

Is history made by those with a sense of style? The real question is, can it be unmade by those without a sense of style?

"By combining subjectivity and objectivity, one is able to reach the state of nothingness. It is a battle against oneself," says a character in the long-running Japanese samurai TV show, *Lone Wolf and Cub. The* same combination is necessary, of course, to realize the nothingness of the State. But how?

As a transcriptionist, I typed up medical chart notes in the SOAP format with four headings: Subjective, Objective, Assessment and Plan. Under the first, the patient describes how they're feeling; under the second, the physician records what they're seeing; under the third, possible diagnoses are noted, and under the fourth, steps to be taken are listed.

John never ignores the subjective dimensions of current alienation, even while objectively tracing the reach and extent of that alienation. Here "Animal Dreams" in particular deepens a feeling of animal kinship by objectively presenting the best evidence of animal intelligence.

Yet most importantly, John provides an assessment. Early on it was recognized that "where there is no vision, the people perish." (Prov. 29:18)

The best assessments are simplest. John's assessment, it seems to me, is simply this: civilization is of no interest, ultimately.

The best plans, too, are simple. John's dismissal of civilization makes it that much easier not to dismiss traditional indigenous resistance. Can there be a better plan than putting First Peoples first?

Can there be a better plan than seeing the world in front of our faces? If rebellion is to be something more than mythical, perhaps it will realize itself through myth. In the myth of the Trojan War, the goddesses of Power, Wisdom and Pleasure dispute who is most beautiful.

Eventually Paris, a herdsman known for his scrupulously fair judgments, is asked to choose. He chooses the goddess of Pleasure, and thus sets in motion the events leading to the Trojan War. His choice of Pleasure brings him the displeasure of the other goddesses, who forever after hate him, but never is he abandoned by his goddess:

"Aphrodite, who loves all smiling lips and eyes,
cleaves to her man to ward off peril from him.
He thought he faced death, but she saved him."
The Iliad, Book IV, Lines 9–11

This myth suggests each of us can choose inspiration from Power, Wisdom, or Pleasure, and that no matter what we choose, we can't have it all. Yet where within contemporary society is there anything remotely resembling Power, Wisdom or Pleasure?

If we find these, it will only be through supporting traditional indigenous resistance. Traditional indigenous people are still here; traditional indigenous people are still connected to the Earth. Civilized people have made that connection tenuous but have never broken it and never will.

For non-indigenous people, the critical issue was defined as constancy by Jonathan Kozol in his bleak and unsparing assessment of why the uprisings in the 1960s failed. In The Night is Dark and I Am Far from Home, *he wondered what loyalties could be constructed on a groundwork of desertion:*

"There is, for each of us, the need to learn and grow, to voyage and explore, above all in the terms of our own consciousness of what "school" is about. [Kozol was an educator.] There is, however, a much deeper need to find one solid core of concrete action and specific dedication, in just one neighborhood, or in one city, with one group of children and one group of allies and one set of loyalties, and with one deep, deep dream of love and transformation."

This is what John has found, and for decades, and many of us around the world are as grateful for his steadfastness as we are for his clarity. Both are unfailing.

Clarity is hardly adequate in undoing our conditioning, but such re-wilding, if you will, can hardly hope to get very far without clarity. John has made abundantly clear how little can be expected from projects which do not explicitly reject domestication and civilization. That in itself clears the way for what might constitute a threat to the relations of unreality that have really enslaved us for far too long.

Lang Gore
Author of *Hunting Seasons*

WHY

HOPE?

PART I: ORIGINS

These offerings range from remote, even abstract, origins to a more recent historical case study. Looking at the roots of our present condition is salutary, as I see it, even required. Some argue that any focus on prehistory or history only detracts from one's radical subjectivity–supposedly the world's only true source of resistance in itself. In my opinion, those who fail to examine origins cut themselves off from grasping how our captivity arrived, how it works, and what alternatives have existed.

In the Beginning

A LINGERING SENSE OF ORIGIN continues to lay claim to our hearts and minds. It beckons because we have been exiled from something. Odysseus seeks a return in his Odyssey and in fact there may be no older figure in Western civilization than the wanderer, the pilgrim, the voyager in search of a homecoming. "Where are we going?" asked Novalis, and answered: "Always home."[1]

We are certainly stranded today, more and more so. The perfecting of communication technology, for example, finds us ever more cut off and lonely. Schelling, who like Novalis wrote some two hundred years ago, is helpful here: "…each era has always obscured its predecessor, so that it hardly betrays any sign of an origin…the work of thousands of years must be stripped away to come at last to the foundation, to the ground."[2] Although Progress has carried us far from Origin, it has not disappeared. Cezanne wanted to grasp "nature in its origin";[3] the task of the artist is "to lend duration to genesis [origin]."[4] Unfashionable now perhaps, but as Edward Shils notes, "Some preoccupation with 'origin' is found in almost all human societies."[5]

Origin speaks to us of our goal or destination. Karl Kraus, bluntly: "The origin is the goal."[6] Without interest in it, without a conception of what is involved, there is less of a sense of possible arrival. Origin can help liberate the future insofar as it retrieves our relation to what has come before.

What is it of which we speak? Is it some kind of Big Bang? Fichte wondered whether or not there is "an absolute origin, starting from which and beyond which it is impossible to go further."[7] Event is a popular buzzword in some philosophical circles today. Is origin, at base, a kind of "Event"? Or more of a state of being, a primordial condition (particle or wave)? Rousseau stressed an aboriginal state of nature, which certainly could be a strong candidate. And Paul de Man conceded "the hold it has over our present thought."[8] In his *Remembering Paradise*, Peter Nosco refers to "the remarkable degree of similarity between depictions [of supposed original Golden Ages]…over hundreds if not thousands of years in otherwise radically different societies."[9] Edenic beginnings of humanity, treasured cross-culturally.

There have been and still are those who insist that questions about origin are, or should be, at the heart of mindful endeavor. Even as philosophy overall seems to have decided that "the origin is not available to us."[10] The postmodernists go further still: origin is not only unavailable, its pursuit is wholly misguided and illusory. Having forsaken overview, meaning/truth, clarity, causality and a few other basics, it is unsurprising that origin, too, is part of their craven retreat on all fronts, into word games, cut-rate aesthetics, and relativism. But the often-announced eclipse of postmodernism, by the way, may finally be arriving. One hopeful sign is what is called the new historicism, a cultural materialist outlook with potentially utopian overtones and an interest in origins.[11]

Phenomenology-oriented Eugen Fink provides a caveat: "The more originary the force which ventures to open a clearing, the deeper are the shadows in its fundamental ideas."[12] A provocative warning that will serve to introduce the other side of the coin: origin in a distinctly negative sense.

What is the originary event, the onset, of the disease called civilization? Do we not assume that combating an illness means first finding out what caused it, what explains its progression, its symptoms? For Rene Girard, the foundation was a scapegoating. An act of collective sacrificial violence brought forth civilized humanity. Eric Gans explains it in terms of the birth of symbolic culture. Language, representation itself, is the origin.[13] Gans noticed, *pace* Freud, that the move to the symbolic and its development is at base a continuing renunciation, a continuing loss. I've explored origin as a negative element in various respects, off and on for a few decades. What is the positive draw, the gravitational pull of origin?

Nostalgia may fit a variety of meanings or purposes. As an ideological add-on in the service of an idealized political culture, as a merchandising ploy peddling recycled kitsch, for example. Serving the role of manipulation or sentimentality is not about origin, but there is much more to nostalgia than such categories.

There is a literature that in fact sees it on a deeper level altogether, valorizing nostalgia as a refusal to become accustomed to the present state of misfortune. Janelle Wilson's *Nostalgia* is subtitled *Sanctuary of Meaning*,[14] for instance, and Helmut Illbruck's book on the subject is meant as his "own defense of nostalgia,"[15] as implicit critique of modernity's failed claims. Edward Casey refers to our desire for a homecoming "to which nostalgia, alone in human experience, can introduce us."[16] Ralph Harper's earlier, existential foray finds "the unique power of nostalgic imagination," with his conclusion: "It is meant to be prophetic."[17]

Origin has a unique claim on us, deepened, it seems, by the void we find ourselves in, the immeasurable loss of both freedom and community. Lost authenticity is certified in its absence, in the anguish of separation from it. One notices that there is no negative nostalgia. "When the real is no longer what it was," writes Jean Baudrillard, "nostalgia assumes its full meaning."[18] The felt lack is powerful and persistent, and nostalgia "recurs with a vengeance."[19] It turns to the past because there it finds something of a future that has been forgotten—and should not remain so.

Heidegger saw in a reflective nostalgia the "fundamental tonality" of philosophy.[20] He also wondered whether the feelings of nostalgia may be lost because of the profundity of our disruption and uprootedness. Indeed, it may be possible at times to be nostalgic for being able to be nostalgic. Measuring its proliferation, intensity, ebbs and flows would seem a challenging project.

Nostalgia is thought to have early modern beginnings of significance.[21] By the nineteenth century it was largely thought of as a clinical category, a medical condition. It was not only figures like Hegel and Freud who viewed nostalgia in terms of faulty development, an obstacle to full health. But nostalgia has endured, and faith in Enlightenment has diminished. Nostalgia, somehow more focused and critical, may go forward as more than the guilty conscience of Progress. It has what Ill-bruck termed a "material core,"[22] a real basis, and is needed more than ever in the age of the global postmodern. Nostalgia comes unbidden, an alloy of the lost and the found, unsettling but hinting strongly of deliverance. Can what was once known ever be truly lost?

"Originsland" is where the various takes on the subject reside, according to the playful designation of archaeologist of human origins Clive Gamble. A very slowly emerging objectification of time, most likely fueled by very slowly developing specialization or division of labor, carried us away from origin.[23] "Before the beginning of years,/There came to the making of man/Time with a gift of tears," as Swinburne captured it so well.[24] We know that stone tools were being fashioned almost three million years ago and that symbolic culture is only about 30,000 years old.[25] We clung to some kind of origin, is one way to put it.

Domestication started its reign about 10,000 years ago and the first civilization soon thereafter. The story of the latter may be seen as an ensemble of compensations. Religion, art, conquest, technology, the Left, etc.—all means to overcome or overlook a primary deprivation, to make up for distancing from origin.

Mircea Eliade stressed the regenerative aspect of ritual, its connection to founding events or an original state. Liturgy in general is a symbolism of the originary. In *Dreamtime*, Hans Peter Duerr cited the Wemale of the Moluccas and the African Bembas whose girls celebrate a "return to the origins" in an initiation ceremony during which they crawl backward, as through the birth canal.[26]

Plato, especially in his *Republic*, is oriented quite differently. And in the story of the Cave, origin is likewise a problem to be transcended, not a paradise lost waiting to be regained. In a similar vein, Aristotle divined that slavery and the subjugation of women were ordained to be so from the beginning of society; thus no need to explore origin.

About two millennia later origin was a major topic, with works on the subject by Burke, Condillac, Herder and Rousseau. The latter's *Discourse on the Origins of Inequality* is probably the best known of these eighteenth-century offerings. Immanuel Kant expressed well the Enlightenment attitude toward origin. Unlike Herder and Rousseau, Kant felt any imagined homecoming to be an illusion; the yearning is really just for lost youth. "His strategic use of the tale of origins demands of his readers that they position themselves with him as participants in the ongoing narrative of Enlightenment," in Genevieve Lloyd's fine summing up.[27] That is, endless progress and no need of origin, as a moral duty backed up by law. Kant's anti-origin perspective would be realized in a universal, international urbanism,[28] in which we recognize today's globalized mass society.

Hegel was no more drawn by origin than was Descartes. Kierkegaard believed that existence should recover its eternal primitivity. "If we lacked nothing," he noted, "we should not be overcome with homesickness."[29] John Stuart Mill questioned in passing how much we have gained by civilization.[30]

Nietzsche's early work had been profoundly concerned with the question of origin, but he became very skeptical toward the idea.[31] "Fact"-oriented positivists had nothing in common with Nietzsche in terms of method or style, but their repudiation of inquiry into origins matched his later position. Reversing the sequence, origin becomes present in Hölderlin's later poetry.

In the twentieth century, Paul Valéry tried to tap the point of origin in some of his poems and prose, seeking to recapture an original whole and its promise.[32] Rilke wondered whether "Perhaps creating something is nothing but an act of profound remembrance,"[33] providing a positive version of Adorno and Horkheimer's "Every reification is a forgetting" formulation.[34] Rilke's *Sonnets to Orpheus* provide another gem, "for us existence still can enchant; in a hundred/places it's still origin."[35]

In Walter Benjamin's masterwork, *The Origin of German Tragic Drama*, origin is the central epistemological concept. "Philosophical history, the science of the origin"[36] is the key to this work on the German Baroque. Benjamin also focused on the loss of aura, mass society's banishment of the original, and came finally to ponder the origin of history itself.

Edmund Husserl launched phenomenology as a quest to uncover what is beneath the concept, before reality is captured by words. His pupil, Martin Heidegger, in many ways centered his whole work on origin, which he saw as unthought in philosophy. His term "the Open" bears on this, as a kind of primordial condition or enigma.[37] He described homecoming as "[becoming homely] (*heimlich*–closer to our informal "homey") in nearness to the origin," which he saw not only philosophically but politically. That is, as specifically a German homecoming.[38] This nationalist orientation was surely part of the appeal that National Socialism had for Heidegger, a grotesque application of origin thinking.

Pierre Teilhard de Chardin, a mid-century Catholic partisan of Progress, proclaimed discontinuity and the loss of any point of origin. In this he anticipated the postmodern refusal of causality and stable meaning. Foucault, for example, saw history as discontinuous at every point, such that it "deprives the self of the reassuring stability of life and nature."[39] Of course, it is the actual movement of domination that has undermined this stability, rather than his or anyone else's approach to history. Foucault's outlook is a reflection of and an accommodation to that movement, a rejection of ideas of continuity and causality that are essential to understand and overcome that disastrous current. His compatriot in surrender, Jacques Derrida, was never far from insisting on the wrongness of any search for the originary, nor, similarly, from his unrelenting stress on the impossibility of non-alienation. This weak dead-endism finds its solipsistic extreme with Jean-Luc Nancy: "Each new coming is the origin: the world begins its turn each time with me."[40]

Deleuze and Guattari were firmly against origin. Their most well-known concept is the rhizome, rootless and lying on the surface. "A plateau is always in the middle, not at the beginning or the end. A rhizome is made up of plateaus,"[41] to continue the metaphor. We are thus trapped in a presence-less present, cut off from seeing its source. They second Nietzsche's move from origin to genealogy, from originating critique to mere contingency, foreclosing origin.

Maurice Merleau-Ponty, to the contrary, sought a radical starting point. The originating, he felt, is not behind us (as in out of reach): "Reflection consists in seeking the originating, that by which everything else can be and can be thought."[42] Merleau-Ponty found the basis of origin in the very upsurge of nature, so very unlike the many who have recognized only what is *not* nature as a source or ground.

Nostalgia de la Luz (*Nostalgia for the Light*) is a very evocative 2010 film by Chilean director Patricio Guzman. Set in the high Atacama Desert, the film's focus alternates between the astronomers who gaze into the heavens in search of the beginnings of the universe, and the women who scour the desert in hopes of finding remains of their loved ones, who were murdered by the Pinochet regime and dumped in this remote area. I am not privy to Guzman's possible intentions, but his excellent documentary might be seen as a metaphor for our situation as a whole. We may long to connect with origin, but we also contend with the dire realities so much closer at hand.

The way the story begins must have a lot to do with how it ends. There was a Fall into all this, into the foundations of modernity, inaugurated by symbolic culture and domestication. And before that?

What we have forgotten may be recovered. Unfolding origin, a journey to origins, is possible. Every authentic choice takes us nearer. We feel the pull to be present, directly and fully, to ourselves and the world. Odysseus is always only heading back to Ithaca.

(ENDNOTES)

1   Quoted in Peter Sloterdijk, *Spheres. Volume 1: Bubbles Microspherology* (Los Angeles: Semiotext(e), 2011), p. 56.

2   Quoted in Alan Cardew, "The Archaic and the Sublimity of Origins," in Paul Bishop, ed., *The Archaic: The Past in the Present* (New York: Routledge, 2012), p. 122.

3   Maurice Merleau-Ponty, *Sens et Non-Sens*, translated and quoted in Gary Brent Madison, *The Phenomenology of Merleau-Ponty* (Athens, OH: Ohio University Press, 1981), p. 75.

4   Quoted in Jean Gebser, *The Ever-Present Origin* (Athens, OH: Ohio University Press, 1985), p. 484.

5   Edward Shils, *Tradition* (Chicago: University of Chicago Press, 1981), p. 235.

6   Quoted in Theodor W. Adorno, *Negative Dialectics* (New York: Continuum, 1997), p. 155.

7   Bishop, *op.cit.,* introduction, p. 14.

8   Paul de Man, *Allegories of Reading* (New Haven: Yale University Press, 1979), p. 136.

9   Peter Nosco, *Remembering Paradise: Nativism and Nostalgia in Eighteenth-Century Japan* (Cambridge, MA: Council on East Asian Studies, Harvard University, 1990), p. 5.

10 Ugo Perone, *The Possible Present* (Albany: State University of New York Press, 2011), p. 94.

11 See Amy J. Elias, "Faithful Historicism and Philosophical Semi-Retirement," in Allen Dunn and Thomas F. Haddox, *The Limits of Literary Historicism* (Knoxville: The University of Tennessee Press, 2010), for an example of bitter postmodern hostility to the new historicism.

12 Quoted in Dana Hollander, *Exemplarity and Chosenness* (Stanford: Stanford University Press, 2008), p. 80.

13 Eric Gans, *Signs of Paradox* (Stanford: Stanford University Press, 1997), e.g. pp. 131–137.

14 Janelle L. Wilson, *Nostalgia: Sanctuary of Meaning* (Lewisburg, PA: Bucknell University Press, 2005).

15 Helmut Illbruck, *Nostalgia: Origins and Ends of an Unenlightened Disease* (Evanston, IL: Northwestern University Press, 2012), p. 160.

16 Edward S. Casey, "The World of Nostalgia," *Man and World* 20 (1987), p. 380.

17 Ralph Harper, *Nostalgia* (Cleveland, OH: The Press of Western Reserve University, 1966), p. 16.

18 Quoted in Illbruck, *op.cit.*, p. 24.

19 *Ibid.*, p. 183.

20 Quoted in Sylviane Agacinski, *Time Passing: Modernity and Nostalgia* (New York: Columbia University Press, 2003), p. 17.

21 Louis A. Ruprecht, *Afterwards: Hellenism, Modernism, and the Myth of Decadence* (Albany: State University of New York Press, 1996), p. 36.

22 Illbruck, *op.cit.*, p. 251.

23 Regarding the symbolic dimension of time as possibly the original alienation, see my "Beginning of Time, End of Time" in *Elements of Refusal* (Columbia, MO: C.A.L. Press, 1999) and "Time and its Discontents" in *Running on Emptiness: The Pathology of Civilization* (Los Angeles: Feral House, 2002).

24 Algernon Charles Swinburne, "Before the Beginning of Years," in Terry L. Myers, "Before the Beginning of Years: A Swinburne Curiosity," *Victorian Poetry* 37:4 (Winter 1999), p. 546.

25 Cognition is a precondition of language, not a consequence of its emergence. José Luis Bermùdez, *Thinking Without Words* (New York: Oxford University Press, 2003), pp. 4–5.

26 Hans Peter Duerr, *Dreamtime: Concerning the Boundary between Wilderness and Civilization* (New York: Basil Blackwell, 1985), p. 71.

27 Genevieve Lloyd, *Providence Lost* (Cambridge, MA: Harvard University Press, 2008), p. 295.

28 *Ibid.*, p. 292.

29 Quoted in Harper, *op.cit.*, p. 141.

30 Michael Levin, *J.S. Mill on Civilization and Barbarism* (New York: Routledge, 2004), p. 26.

31 Bishop, *op.cit.*, pp. 17–18.

32 See Kirsteen Anderson, *Paul Valéry and the Voice of Desire* (Oxford: European Humanities Research Centre, 2000), e.g. pp. 25, 103, 107.

33 Rainer Maria Rilke, *The Poet's Guide to Life* (New York: Modern Library, 2005), p. 45.

34 Theodor Adorno and Max Horkheimer, *Dialectic of Enlightenment* (New York: Continuum, 1986), p. 230.

35 Quoted in Stephanie Dowrick, *In the Company of Rilke* (New York: Jeremy P. Tarcher/Penguin, 2011), p. 21.

36 Walter Benjamin, *The Origin of German Tragic Drama* (New York: Verso, 1998), p. 47.

37 Carol Bigwood, *Earth Muse: Feminism, Nature, and Art* (Philadelphia: Temple University Press, 1993), pp. 35–36.

38 Bishop, *op.cit.*, p. 162.

10.

39 Quoted in H.D. Hartoonian, "Foucault, Genealogy, History: The Pursuit of Otherness," in Jonathan Arac, ed., *After Foucault* (New Brunswick, NJ: Rutgers University Press, 1988), p. 121.

40 Jean-Luc Nancy, *Being Singular Plural* (Stanford: Stanford University Press, 1999), p. 19.

41 Quoted in Gregory Flaxman, *Gilles Deleuze and the Fabulation of Philosophy* (Minneapolis: University of Minnesota Press, 2012), p. 1.

42 Quoted in Madison, *op.cit.*, p. 155.

Numb and Number

The digital age is pre-eminently the ultimate reign of Number. The time of Big Data, computers (e.g. China's, world's fastest) that can process thirty quadrillion transactions per second, algorithms that increasingly predict—and control—what happens in society. Standardized testing is another example of the reductive disease of quantification.

Number surpasses all other ideas for its combination of impact and implication. Counting means imposing a definition and a control, assigning a number value. It is the foundation for a world in which whatever can be domesticated and controlled can also be commodified. Number is the key to mastery: everything must be measured, quantified. It is not what we can do with number, but what it does to us. Like technology, its intimate ally, number is anything but neutral. It tries to make us forget that there is so much that shouldn't or can't be measured.

Fifth Estate published my "Number: Its Origin and Evolution" in Summer 1985, just as the digital age was gaining traction following the personal computer explosion at the beginning of the '80s.[1] The quickening (anti-) pulse of technological change over the past thirty years has been at base a mathematization. Social life in the post-community era is detached, disembodied, drained, statistical. Its core is administration, just as the essence of number is calculation. "Mathematical thinking is coercive," disclosed British philosopher J.R. Lucas.[2] Number totalizes; in mathematics, ambiguity is anathema. The technoculture obeys these norms, and we dance to its tune, its code: number.

But there are some who applaud the new, always more arid reality. And postmodernism wasn't the nadir of thought, after all. Alain Badiou denies that the Techno Age brings more and more nihilism and mediocrity. Mocking Heidegger's critique of the ascendancy of technology, he declares that there's not enough of it![3]

Badiou's *Being and Event* (1988), empty and ahistorical, somehow installed him as arguably the biggest star of philosophy in the West. *Number and Numbers* (1990) is his follow-up hymn to estrangement.[4] Mathematics is philosophy, is being, in a formulation as hideous as it is astounding. Fellow Marxist-Leninist and postmodern/speed freak/pop culture clown Slavoj Zizek proclaimed *Number and Numbers* "breath-taking...[it] announces a new epoch in philosophy."[5] Zizek is correct, but only in a thoroughly negative sense. Michel Foucault evidently didn't see Badiou coming when he held that "theory is by nature opposed to power."[6]

Number implies a relationship and that relationship is precisely that of power, as with capital, but more primary. Communists like Badiou (and Zizek), needless to say, have never taken the trouble to oppose power. A footnote by Andrew Gibson is revealing. Badiou had told him "that he has no liking for James Joyce. One suspects that there is simply too much world there for him."[7] Too much uncontrolled world?

Number is a form of being for Badiou. What's more, "mathematics is the infinite development of what can be said of being *qua* being."[8] That is, mathematics is already philosophy; ontology is actually mathematics.

Postmodernism elevated liberal doubt as its response to anyone who could imagine a condition outside alienation and subjection. It worked in a negative vein (e.g. Derrida) to undermine any grounds for hope. Badiou promotes a positivity that works toward the same end. For him, politics is the possibility of a "rupture with what exists."[9] But he grounds this positive hope, his "rupture," in what couldn't possibly be more a part of alienation and subjection. Badiou translator Jason Barker notes correctly: "Badiou's canonical politico-philosophical reference point is Althusser's *Lenin and Philosophy and Other Essays*."[10] The Stalinist Althusser supported the French Communist Party against the workers and students of the May '68 uprising. As Badiou freely admits, "there is no theory of the subject in Althusser, nor could there ever be one."[11] Two communists joining hands against the individual, against liberation. What is "seemingly phrased in strictly mathematical language," as Bruno Bosteels sees it, "is imported from the realm of militant politics." Specifically the Marxist-Leninist versions of such categories, such as "normality, singularity, and excrescence."[12] Even more specifically, Maoism.

Francois Laruelle finds that Badiou's "enterprise has no equivalent in the history of philosophy," a fusion of Platonist mathematicism and Maoism."[13] "Thought" at its most nakedly authoritarian on every level.

Platonism vis-à-vis math means that numbers are independently existing objects. But numbers are not out there, somewhere, to be discovered;

they are invented, as Wittgenstein, for one, grasped quite well. Invented to meet the needs of complex, unequal societies. Counting, accounting, a growing obsession that began with domestication and civilization, has reached the point, according to Ellul, where "everything in human life that does not lend itself to mathematical treatment must be excluded."[14]

We can count and measure only the lifeless because such processes necessarily exclude what is living. The noted nineteenth-century mathematician Gottlob Frege proclaimed "the miracle of number" but also stated that "the highest degree of [mathematical] rigor...is at the furthest remove from what is natural."[15] As Thoreau put it succinctly, "Nature so abhors a straight line."[16]

Philosopher of science Keith Devlin is wrong to aver that numbers "arise from the recognition of patterns in the world around us."[17] They arise because they are necessary for running a certain kind of society; numbers have only an imposed relationship to what is found in the world. Math historian Graham Flegg makes a similar error when he asserts, "Numbers reveal the unity which underlies all of life as we experience it."[18] The "unity" in question did not exist before it was produced, with the invaluable assistance of number.

In Badiou's nonsensical formulation, mathematics is "the history of eternity."[19] It is considerably saner to notice that the development of math is intimately involved with the development of the whole of civilization. On the heels of domestication (and its progeny, private property), grain needed weighing for sale, and land needed surveying for ownership—and soon enough, for taxation. Geometry, after all, is literally "land measurement." Organization and engineering certainly required the services of Egyptian and Babylonian mathematics to enable the first two civilizations in the West.

It is no coincidence that it was the Babylonian/Sumerian civilization, the first real empire, which first developed the idea of written numbers.[20] Number is key to large-scale management and mobilization; numbers and empire have gone hand in hand since earliest times. Babylonian arithmetic was "fully articulated as an abstract computational science by about 2000 B.C.,"[21] about two thousand years before the famed "classical" mathematics of the Greeks.

"All is number," announced Pythagoras, who thereby founded a religion, it should be added. Plato, a Pythagorean, composed the soul from seven numbers in his *Timaeus*. And in India as well as in Greece, certain exacting ritual requirements were specified by geometrical exercises intended to avert suffering at the hands of the gods.[22] Nor has this form of idealism died out; the twentieth-century mathematician-philosopher L.E.J. Brouwer regarded the universe as "a construction of the mathematician."[23]

It was the wealthy, aristocratic Plato who famously asserted the ontological primacy of math, which Badiou unreservedly seconds. A corollary is that for Plato, the first upward steps out of the cave toward wisdom begin with mastery of the arts of number. This put thought on the path of representation and mathematical objectification. Mathematics' more concrete, everyday role—to serve the needs of power—makes this path the history of oppression, rather than Badiou's "history of eternity."

Badiou approvingly quotes the German mathematician Richard Dedekind to the effect that "man is always counting."[24] Of course it is well-established that in most primal communities people use only "one, two, many" as the limit of their interest in number. In a recent example, Daniel Everett, referring to his years in Amazonian Brazil, concludes that "the **Pirahã** have no number at all and no counting in any form."[25]

Let us also add a qualification about the use of numbers. Ethnographer W.J. McGee judged that aboriginal people "commonly see in numbers qualities or potencies not customarily recognized by peoples of more advanced culture."[26] The association or coloration used with numbers means that they had not yet lost their sense of the uniqueness of everything, every event. This is still present with early terms of measurement. The units—such as the yard, the foot, the pound—were of human size and reference, and local relevance, until mass long-distance civilization took over.

Negative numbers came of age in the latter half of the Middle Ages. They were of inestimable assistance with larger financial transactions in which there might be net losses. At this time international banking greatly expanded, giving math a new value.[27] Well before Galileo, Copernicus, and Descartes provided the Faustian underpinnings for number's cardinal role in dominating nature, math had already become essential for merchants, cartographers, imperial navigators, bankers, and others.

The Scientific Revolution, chiefly of the 1600s, largely revolved around the spirit of number. In 1702 Fontenelle observed that the "geometric spirit" is required if order and precision are to be established.[28] This spirit bloomed with Immanuel Kant (1724–1804). Knowledge for him is mathematical knowledge. Necessary and *a priori*, already always present, number is central to all the categories of our cognitive process. The new prominence of the mathematical infected society at large. Enlightenment thinkers spoke of a comprehensive "geometry of politics," a "social mathematics."[29]

In his *Description of New England* (1616), Captain John Smith asked native individuals how many fish they caught, in order to more accurately gauge the level of potential plunder. He found that "the Savages compare their store in the sea to the haires of their heads,"[30] most likely an unsatisfactory report. Obsession with a mathematical orientation was present in North America early on but was not pervasive until the 1820s, according to Patricia Cohen. Her *A Calculating People* focused on "the sudden popularity of numbers and statistics in Jacksonian America."[31]

Counting consists of assigning words to things. The first counting symbols were, in fact, the first writing. At this early stage many cultures expressed letters and numbers by the same symbols. Aleph, for example, expressed both the first letter of the Hebrew alphabet and the first of the ordinal numbers.[32] Spengler pushed the connection much further, wondering whether with number one finds "the birth of grammar."[33]

Measurement, like counting, deals with just one aspect of the object it is measuring and assigns a number to that aspect. This abstracting move is basic to the universal standardization of life inherent in globalizing civilization. Of course, there is and always has been resistance. But in the words of psychologist S.S. Stevens, "Given the deeply human need to quantify, could mathematics really have begun elsewhere than in measurement?"[34] In a similar vein, John Henslow found that "measurement is what defines humanity…is what distinguishes the civilized from the uncivilized."[35]

Growing social complexity and the all-encompassing integration required by modern domination means more and more measurement. It is as ubiquitous as it is imposed. "A deeply human need"—or the dynamic of ruinous civilization? There is no civilization without measurement, but there is life outside civilization—and ultimately, perhaps *only* outside civilization.

The prevailing view is that knowledge is limited without measurement, that we can't really grasp something unless it can be measured.

The word "grasp" is telling; it belongs to the language of control. To control, dominate, and hold nature in our grasp, for example: the lexicon of domestication. Is this really a way of understanding? What is lost when we only measure? Does this approach not take us away from a more intimate knowing? Traditional indigenous people do not "grasp" in their knowing.

A small instance from the realm of "fitness": e-devices with their apps for measuring bodily performance as a function of various rates: breath, pulse, etc. A way of externalizing and objectifying our own bodies, of losing touch with ourselves and our senses.

This is part of the growing technification and concomitant deskilling, hallmarks of the digital age. Ironically, this movement does not produce greater proficiency in numbers. Numeracy, in fact, is in decline. Computers have replaced cash registers; retail clerks have no need to make change, and many don't know how. A friend, when asked for the time by a teenager, pointed to a nearby clock. The teen couldn't tell time from a clockface, only a digital readout.

Inevitably asked for a definition of time, that always-elusive question, Einstein replied that it's what a clock measures. The correspondence between measurement and time has been much discussed; but in what does the measuring of time consist?

Plato found an intrinsic connection between time and number, but that only reminds us that we can't be sure what kind of things time and number are. Aristotle claimed that things are in time the way what is counted is in number, as if that clarifies matters much.

In the third century A.D. Plotinus asked, "Why should the mere presence of a number give us Time?"[36] Which is suggestive, in terms of how time stakes its claim, and prompts a closer look at timekeeping itself. Consider seventh-century Bedouins in what is now Saudi Arabia. Though pastoral (and therefore domesticators), they had a very minimal sense of time. Along came Mohammad, who unveiled time as part of a new religion. Five compulsory prayer times regulated each day. All our days, said the Prophet, are numbered, just as math-guided industrial processes would regulate and number them a millennium later.

For the Mayans and others in Mesoamerica, a focus on time and number mirrored a preoccupation with order and rule. Bergson's *durée*, or lived time, was an attempt to step outside of imposed, identically numbered time. But the bond between time and number has continued and deepened, as domesticating reality commandeers more and more places and lives on the planet.

"There is no way we can escape from numbers," concluded Graham Flegg.[37] Philosopher Michel Serres agreed: "Wherever the road of mathematicity was opened, it was forever."[38] The same unending servitude is consecrated by Badiou, who stakes thought itself on number. But we may imagine what could emerge when the counting and measuring and timing is over, by our own ending of it. Imagine what could emerge only in such a world.

The "elegance" of math? Much more akin to the coldness of advanced civilization. Political theorist Susan Buck-Morss expressed this with great eloquence: "The social body of civilization is impersonal, indifferent to that fellow-feeling that within a face-to-face society causes its members to act with moral concern."[39] Face to face, where there is little or no need of counting.

Dedekind said that numbers "are a means of apprehending more easily and more sharply the difference of things."[40] What difference could he have been referring to? The written numbering systems of the ancient Egyptians, Hittites, Greeks, and Aztecs were structurally identical,[41] and this congruence pointed toward the global homogenization so strongly underway now.

A hollowed-out mathematical order is that of closed-off coldness, indifference, cynicism. The rise in the incidence of autism is one sad aspect among many; it may be worth noting that a disproportionate number of math students and theorists have received a diagnosis of autism.[42]

Number trumps quality and qualities; meanwhile Badiou bases his authoritarianism on the deepest grounding for massification and estrangement. Healthy individuals avoid such brutalist "thinkers." The second-century physician Galen provides a cautionary tale: "It has often happened that people have talked happily with me, because of my work among the sick, but when they discover that I am also an expert mathematician, they avoid me."[43]

(ENDNOTES)

1   Available in John Zerzan, *Elements of Refusal* (Columbia, MO: C.A.L. Press/Paleo Editions, 1998.

2   J.R. Lucas, *The Conceptual Roots of Mathematics* (New York: Routledge, 2000), p. 20.

3   Alain Badiou, *Manifesto for Philosophy* (Albany: State University of New York, 1999), e.g. pp. 54, 57.

4   Alain Badiou, *Number and Numbers* (Malden, MA: Polity, 2008).

5   *Ibid.*, cover blurb.

6   Quoted in Gary Gutting, *Thinking the Impossible* (New York: Oxford University Press, 2011), p. 20.

7   Andrew Gibson, *Intermittency* (Edinburgh: Edinburgh University Press, 2012), p. 67.

8   Alain Badiou, *Conditions* (New York: Continuum, 2008), p. 111.

9   Alain Badiou, *Metapolitics* (New York: Verso, 2005), p. 24.

10 *Ibid.*, p. xxix.

11 *Ibid.*, p. 59.

12 Bruno Bosteels, *Badiou and Politics* (Durham, NC: Duke University Press, 2011), p. 39.

13 Francois Laruelle, *Anti-Badiou* (New York, Bloomsbury, 2013), pp. vii, viii.

14 Jacques Ellul, *The Technological Society* (New York: Alfred A. Knopf, 1964), p. 431.

15 Gottlob Frege, *Posthumous Writings* (Chicago: The University of Chicago Press, 1979), p. 146.

16 Henry David Thoreau, *The Writings of Henry David Thoreau*, vol. 9 (Journal entry, February 27, 1857) (Boston: Houghton Mifflin, 1906), p. 281.

17 Keith Devlin, *Mathematics: The Science of Patterns* (New York: Scientific American Library, 1994), p. 9.

18 Graham Flegg, *Numbers: Their History and Meaning* (New York: Schocken Books, 1983), p. 5.

19 Badiou, *Number and Numbers*, p. 214.

20 David Boyle, *The Tyranny of Numbers* (London: Harper Collins, 2000), p. 7.

21 Charles J. Brainerd, *The Origins of the Number Concept* (New York: Praeger Publishers, 1979), p. 6.

22 B.L. van de Waerden, *Geometry and Algebra in Ancient Civilizations* (New York: Springer-Verlag, 1983), p. 13.

23 Mark von Atten, *Brouwer Meets Husserl* (Dordrecht: Springer, 2007), p. 6.

24 Badiou, *Number and Numbers*, p. 215.

25 Daniel Everett, *Don't Sleep, There are Snakes* (New York: Pantheon Books, 2008), p. 117.

26 W.J. McGee, "Primitive Numbers" in *Nineteenth Annual Report of the Bureau of American Ethnology to the Secretary of the Smithsonian Institution*, Part 2 (Washington, DC: Government Printing Office, 1900), p. 825.

27 See Frank J. Swetz, *Capitalism and Arithmetic* (La Salle, IL: Open Court, 1987).

28 William Leiss, *The Domination of Nature* (Boston: Beacon Press, 1974), p. 78.

29 *Ibid.*, p. 141.

30 Patricia Cline Cohen, *A Calculating People: The Spread of Numeracy in Early America* (Chicago: The University of Chicago Press, 1982), p. 51.

31 *Ibid.*, p. ix.

32 Karl Menninger, *Number Words and Number Symbols* (Cambridge, MA: The M.I.T. Press, 1969), p. 298.

33 Oswald Spengler, *The Decline of the West* Volume II (New York: Alfred A. Knopf, 1928), p. 146.

34 Quoted in John M. Henshaw, *Does Measurement Measure Up?* (Baltimore: The Johns Hopkins University Press, 2006), p. 15.

35 *Ibid.*, p. 280.

36 Quoted in Charles M. Sherover, *The Human Experience of Time* (New York: New York University Press, 1975), p. 73.

37 Flegg, *op.cit.*, p. 1.

38 Michel Serres, *Detachment* (Athens, OH: Ohio University Press, 1989), p. 61.

39 Susan Buck-Morss, "Envisioning Capital: Political Economy on Display," *Critical Inquiry* 21:2 (1995), p. 452.

40 Richard Dedekind, *Essays on the Theory of Numbers* (New York: Dover Publications, 1963), p. 31.

41 Georges Ifrah, *The Universal History of Numbers* (New York: John Wiley & Sons, 1998), p. xx.

42 Michael Fitzgerald and Joan James, *The Mind of the Mathematician* (Baltimore: The Johns Hopkins University Press, 2007), p. 60.

43 J.C. McKeown, *A Cabinet of Greek Curiosities* (Oxford: Oxford University Press, 2013), p. 167.

Origins of the One Percent: The Bronze Age

With the Neolithic Age we entered the force field of domestication, leaving—not without a struggle—the free, face-to-face world of band society/community. Ever-larger settlements, more work, the emergence of warfare and the objectification of women were among the hallmarks of the new order, starting about 10,000 years ago.

But the new era was unstable, domination far from perfected. Sedentary, agriculture-based life posed unforeseen challenges in social, economic, ideological/political, and spiritual spheres. The move from personalized Paleolithic reciprocity to bulk Neolithic resource acquisition, production, and distribution was far from smooth. New modes were needed for domestication to become civilization.

The transition from foraging to farming is widely recognized as the most profound revolution in human history. It is the revolution *into* history, and must have commanded a completely new set of responses to a newly inhabited reality. For one thing, direct, consensual decision-making no longer worked among the burgeoning populations of early complex society. A new level of control and management had to be established. Politics began. Appropriate mental frameworks had to be forged for an increasingly stratified social existence to function. And domestication brought, for the first time, devastating epidemics that resulted from crowded, stationary settlements, along with greatly reduced health and robustness overall. Out of this wrenching defeat, according to Jacques Cauvin, came "all the existential malaises" usually thought of as much later developments.[1]

We know that given a choice, humans prefer to remain hunters and gatherers; we do not settle permanently into the toil of farming until it is forced upon us. The triumph of the Neolithic was that forcing. But domination is not inexorably or invariably linear and unidirectional, and by about 6000 B.C. the Neolithic order was beginning to fray.

Upon its ruins the Bronze Age slowly emerged, with a marked acceleration in social complexity: larger communities tending toward structured social stratification. The challenge was to engineer a new consolidation of authority to counter the social fragmentation that had occurred. The overall Neolithic ideology and its ritual structures needed replacing.[2] For example, a sense of individual property had not yet replaced the community sense of property (e.g. the persistence of village herds). A second Agricultural Revolution—the Bronze Age—was required to draw (or re-draw) and more thoroughly enforce divisions and boundaries: to anchor domestication.[3]

The first civilizations are based on the solutions to such challenges, on success at channeling energies into an altogether new scale of organization (e.g. cities), of rulership, aggression, militarism, and empire-building. Fertility, a staple of domestication, was expanded into great symbolic importance in all early civilizations.

As daily life grew harder, religion presented distant horizons of happiness. Belief in an enhanced life after death appears to have been stronger in territorial states than in city-state systems.[4] Stronger, that is, as political power extended itself.

Theocratic classes served as new organizing authorities, while the deities themselves reflected the always advancing principle of specialization. Each had his or her allotted sphere and role. The gods needed the service of monarchs and priestly bailiffs to execute religious requirements. But despite the divine sanction or legitimation accorded to political figures, they were not immune from assassination, and the threat of violence was needed to collect taxes in early civilizations.

Art and architecture partook of the growing social complexity, reflecting the developing class hierarchy and performing ideological, social-regulatory functions. Spectacle was a new cultural component, making its appearance early on in the service of social integration. Public performance, like ritual, was often highly regimented or structured, and thus paralleled the authoritarian relations closing in among people. As John Baines observes, "It is difficult to imagine any but the smallest-scale and least differentiated society that would exist without some sort of spectacle."[5]

Another ideological support for domestication was the emerging time-consciousness that seems to have accompanied ever-increasing division of labor. In its cruder, public form, the evidence shows that all regimes of early civilizations bureaucratically commandeered time, from Stonehenge-type time computers at the beginning of the Bronze Age to the calendars that regulated official cycles and events.

Literacy is exactly congruent with state formation; the one develops in parallel with the other. As written signs take precedence over memory, a ruling version of reality can be made. Writing provided a great instrument to power and is not only, in Stanley Diamond's words, "one of the original mysteries of civilization," but also its "compulsive rite."[6]

For the past thousand years in the Western world, history has been divided into modern and pre-modern. As distant in time from the Greek and Roman eras as we are today, the Bronze Age is certainly buried in the pre-modern. But as we think our present-day, modern thoughts, how different are they, really, from those thoughts in the first, Bronze Age civilizations? How many deep habits of mind, institutions, routines, go back to the Bronze Age and its brand new spirit and ethos? Was that not the origin of the notion, so basically corrosive to autonomy and freedom, that inequality and hierarchy are normal conditions and that misfortune is not a social evil but an individual's just desserts? A notion so obviously still with us. The Bronze Age devised a mechanical order several millennia before sophisticated power-driven machinery, a stratified order that is "the basic exploitation system which has lasted until the present day."[7]

Early on, what Marx called "domestic" or household industry was already market-oriented, and the consensus is that overall, the Bronze Age was a market economy.[8] Long-distance trade, occupational/full-time specialization, supply/demand-determined prices, capital investment, credit, and other "modern" features are observable by the fourth millennium B.P. Such capitalist aspects have existed in all the civilized countries of the world for as far back as economic evidence can take us. Sam Lilley saw pottery as "the first mechanized production industry, the first step on the way to the mass production factory of today."[9]

Extraction and smelting of metal ores was a principal motor of Bronze Age society, with metallurgy stimulating all other productive activities.[10] Childe found that "modern science and industry…go back to the period when bronze was the dominant industrial metal."[11] By this time, production was taking place well outside the house, and moving from luxury goods for temple and palace elites toward mass consumption.

Theodore Wertime has suggested that the principal cause of deforestation was the demands of ancient metallurgy.[12] Of course, land was also cleared for agriculture, especially after the appearance of new inventions such as the plow. Vast forests (of date palms and many other trees) were eradicated across the Near East.

From an earlier self-sufficiency to a growing dependence on experts, technological complexity brought a division of the self into narrowing roles. One's skills were no longer relatively interchangeable, as they had been in a more egalitarian society. Social class derives from this most basic division; despite Marxist claims, class society did not originate with modern industrial society. It was there very early on and was institutionalized by civilization. The individual was enfeebled, fractionalized, without the understanding or control he/she had in smaller, less complex communities. Society moved away from its constituents, became opaque, something beyond the life of the individual: the path to urban civilization, emerging after 4000 B.C.

Slavery, nonetheless, was "less extensive and oppressive than in many later preindustrial societies," in Bruce Trigger's judgment.[13] Marxists are wrong to assert that early civilizations were slave-based, as they are in error regarding a more recent formation of social classes than was the case.

People had to "tame" themselves to live in cities, that core component of civilization, and cities couldn't exist without "intensive plant and animal domestication."[14] The taming goes on, of course (e.g. genetic engineering, nanotechnology); control, its working logic, is what maintains and reproduces civilization. In terms of daily life, notes Monica Smith, "there are considerable similarities between modern and ancient cities."[15] It is obvious that we are still faced with the social, ethical, and political problems that urban civilization introduced.

The city was "a completely new kind of settlement."[16] No early civilization, according to Trigger, had an egalitarian village base.[17] The emergent urban identities rested upon an imagined and enforced community, as if communal egalitarian foundations survived, albeit in new forms. New, but grounded upon a highly organized system of production a long time in the making. A whole chain of specialized activities laid the groundwork for and maintained the integration process represented by full-blown cities.

While it is difficult to make inferences about ideology from archaeological evidence, it seems valid to see routine activities as the most basic component of a minimum of social cohesion and stability. Technology, especially in its organizational sense, is never outside culture. Division of labor is itself a "technology" of social domination. Robert McC. Adams thus found cultural/political complexity to be "essentially technological,"[18] and is this different today?

To the discipline based on routine must be added other civilizational forces. Referring to the early Bronze Age in Syria, Lebanon, and Palestine, James Mellaart found a very characteristic feature of urbanization in a "gradual uniformity of culture."[19] Heidegger saw here a threat of "destructive error"[20] that cities bring to thought.

When a city, dependent on its surroundings as every city is, has imposed its control over a region, it is thereby a "state." A city must guarantee the inputs required for its survival, must police its trade arteries, and this is the near-universal process in state formation (and war). Civilizations commonly evolve from city-states to territorial states, and finally, to empires.

From the egalitarian world of band society in the Paleolithic there is an evident shift to ranked tribal societies in the Neolithic. The latter often included face-to-face relationships among those of lesser and greater power, within small-scale networks. But "all the qualitative components of the state were already present to some degree among advanced chiefdoms," in Marvin Harris' words.[21] Developed chiefdoms were not unlike simple states.

The state uses force, or it cannot be considered a state. A sense of human inadequacy grew apace as expansion and growing differentiation passed well beyond human scale. Gift obligations, for example, were replaced by tribute and the tax collector. And yet, as Trigger concludes, "In all early civilizations, families, wards, and small communities were permitted and even encouraged to manage their own affairs, to a much greater degree than is characteristic of developed industrial societies."[22]

The state and the new authority relations were phenomena unknown to humans for most of our 2.5-million-year history. During the Bronze Age, civilization was imposed as an abnormal condition, locking the door of a social cage that had only been closed, not secured, during the Neolithic.

All civilizations are the institutionalized appropriation by a small ruling elite of most of what is produced by the submerged classes. Their political/legal structures frequently claim to serve their subjects, but of course, then as now, they exist to protect the privileged position of a few. Punishments enacted by early states, though often cruel by modern standards, do not reflect the strength of law enforcement. They are better understood as testimony to the weakness of coercive authority, its need for drastic measures.

It was once thought that palaces and temples defined Bronze Age life, but this was due to the preponderance of evidence from such sources. More recently, artifacts from other institutions and groups have shed light on other important participants and factors. For instance, urban centers led to accelerated consumption by individuals, in dense networks of interaction. Later, in the Iron Age, Rome became known as the ultimate "consumer city," but the movement in that direction was underway well before. The grid plan of urban design is also associated with Rome, but many of the oldest known cities were built on those lines.[23]

As Michael Mann noted, "All civilizations of recorded history have engaged routinely in highly organized and bloody warfare."[24] Civilizations began in violence and were extended via imperialism. Warrior society was a defining Bronze Age feature, serving to deflect internal contradictions and conflicts outward into territorial expansion. The military offered some upward mobility for those at the bottom, for instance.

According to Homer, this was an age of heroes and their long-distance quests. Most famously, the *Odyssey* recounts years of travel by Odysseus, a classical myth of the Trojan War (fourteenth century B.C.). A warrior elite fostered an ideology of heroic war leaders, complete with the Middle Bronze Age invention of the chariot. Militarism expanded the range of political control, and represented the most obvious phenomenon of all civilizations: patriarchy. Originating in the goal of conquering nature (domestication), society was increasingly "a man's world."[25] Virility now became a cardinal virtue.[26]

Especially very recently there is much public discussion about globalization, about our supposedly rather new global interconnectedness and interdependence. But it is actually "strikingly old,"[27] not much newer than the rise of the earliest cities. A key text is Frank and Gills' *The World System*, which argues that "the contemporary world system has a history of at least 5,000 years."[28] It resulted from the confluence of the hegemonies of Mesopotamia and Egypt, and casts "a strong continuity"[29] with the world of today. William McNeill referred to "the emergence of the original ecumenical world system within which we live today."[30]

Concurrent with the rise of civilization there appears history's first international system, an economically and technologically integrated entity. Andrew and Susan Sherratt maintained that it included such components as "the gold, the skills, the scale, the exotic materials, the sophisticated lifestyle, and the investment capacity."[31] There are varying assessments as to when this globalization was achieved, whether it was earlier or later during the Bronze Age. But the common Marxist perspective, that a world system did not exist before the sixteenth century A.D., clearly misses the mark.

There were many and varied early civilizations on various continents; for example those of north China, Indus Valley India, Mesoamerica, and the Yoruba civilization of west Africa. To focus on civilization and mass society for this brief overview, however, I'll look at the earliest and most studied cases: Mesopotamia and Egypt.

Mesopotamia (roughly contiguous with Iraq) was home to some of the very oldest agricultural settlements. Begun somewhat before 8000 B.C., the domestication process had included most staple crops and herd animals by about 6000 B.C. The Tigris-Euphrates valley, often called the Fertile Crescent, also exhibited social ranking and stratification at least as early as the sixth millennium B.C. More differentials developed among the population, along with manufacturing specialization and administrative bureaucracy, and in the 3000s B.C., the world's earliest known urbanized state societies appeared.

A fundamental premise of Mesopotamian civilization was the "unconditional acceptance of the city as the one and only communal organization."[32] Urbanism was based on the breakdown of simpler, more egalitarian forms of social organization, and the primitive commune was already an anachronism by the Middle Bronze Age.[33] A single-minded city-building policy was a royal aim throughout this entire period, to enact and ensure the pacification of the country. Orlin concluded that the greatest single spur to cities in the Near East was the "forced urbanization of rebellious tribes."[34]

But there were also primary social institutions at work, more basic than that of policy. Justin Jennings observed that "most of the networks that brought goods, people, and ideas to and from the city were outside the control of city administrators."[35] The key, as always, is the prime mover known as division of labor. "Central to all accounts of urbanization or state formation is the concept of specialization," as J.N. Postgate succinctly expresses it.[36]

The urban revolution of the Uruk period, fourth millennium B.C., was a basic reordering of human social life. The first literate urban civilization had fully arrived during the 3000s B.C., borne on a wave of what Robert McC. Adams termed "hyper-developed urbanism."[37] At least half of the Sumerian (south Mesopotamian) population now resided in cities.[38] By around 2500 B.C. even most farmers lived in cities. Another datum that evokes the modern world: smaller families were the rule in cities, larger ones in the villages.[39]

It is the sense of the city, the ideological potency of the urban condition, that is of main importance. In an indirect reference to the uncivilized, seminomadic Amorite tribe, the *Gilgamesh* epic of the early second millennium B.C. introduces Enkidu. He runs wild with the animals until enticed into Uruk in Sumeria, where he becomes domesticated. This key myth, among others, expresses the founding of a civic consciousness that is pervasive in the dominant Mesopotamian literature.[40] The epic poem *Enuma Elish* similarly traces the defeat of pre-civilized chaos by the god Marduk—a task not completed until he establishes the city of Babylon as his abode.[41] In fact, the establishment of a pan-Mesopotamian sensibility is primarily the achievement of triumphant urbanism.

It was the city itself, not forgetting temple and palace as primary power centers, that became the essential aspect of Mesopotamian civilization. A.L. Oppenheim accurately refers to the Mesopotamian city as "the assembly of free citizens."[42] A thousand years before Athens one finds such an institution, with its modern overtones of citizenship and democracy. Arguably, however, it may serve as a reminder that democratic forms have always cloaked the rule of elites. The fact of urbanism in itself seemed to give rise to a concept of citizenship; Thorkild Jacobsen makes a case for "primitive democracy."[43] The persistence of religion, however, reminds us that the context is as far from purely secular-political as it is from pure "democracy."

The official outlook was that humans were servants of the gods, no one more so than the king, who provided justice, ultimately, on behalf of the gods. But in the course of the third millennium B.C., the state ever more transparently assumed the role of the gods and their authority.[44] Religious metaphors continued as the coin of the realm nonetheless. In this sense religion was politics. Even taxation, for example, was couched in religious terms. The distinction among terms such as "religious," "political," and "social" had far less meaning in ancient Mesopotamia than for us today.[45] Functionaries who may have been identifiably "religious" can be found to have played administrative roles in political and economic spheres. At the same time, David and Joan Oates discerned a "basically democratic orientation of society."[46]

This latter city-state ideology or ideal "endured into the first millennium B.C. despite the development of larger states and empires."[47] And despite problematic terminology, Mesopotamian society was becoming more secular; the influence of the temple waned between 2500 and 1500 B.C.[48] Hammurabi, who unified Mesopotamia (ca. 1770s B.C.), promulgated a legendary legal code that espoused a defense of the weak against the strong; it eschewed war and proclaimed tolerance and friendship among peoples. The reality was one of increasing exploitation and expansion,[49] prefiguring modern political rhetoric and the evils it tries to hide or somehow legitimate.

How "archaic" is fealty to authority? Americans sing the national anthem and recite the Pledge of Allegiance. A common custom in Mesopotamia was for the ruler to mold and/or place the first brick for a building project. How like political figures of our time, cutting a ribbon to open a bridge, or digging the first shovelful to begin construction. Political integration, including some of the forms we're used to, began in the Bronze Age.

The Oateses refer to apparent "evidence for strictly observed property rights already in the sixth millennium B.C."[50] By the fourth millennium, division of labor and social stratification are linked to more demand for foreign goods, production of goods for exchange, and capitalization of long-distance trade, according to Norman Yoffee.[51] More specifically, in C.K. Maisel's words, city-states' economies were "structured around 'mass production' (sustained surpluses generated by capital-intensive means), bulk transfers and sophisticated manufacturing—all controlled by rigorous book-keeping that tracked inputs and outputs, profits and losses and overall efficiencies."[52]

Rulers exercised some degree of control over the economic system throughout much of the Bronze Age, but there was a fluctuating relationship between central authority and the private sector. Some craft specialists, for instance, were clients of the centralized institutions, and others were independent. The distinction is not always clear; think of defense contractors in the U.S. today, private corporations entirely dependent on government contracts.

The vocabulary of daily life in Mesopotamia is surprisingly recognizable. Terms for "street" also connote "marketplace," and by about 2000 B.C. the city of Ur, for one, had merchandise-displaying showrooms.[53] "The sophistication of the credit system" at about this time, "including the circulation of debts and titles to real assets as media of exchange is impressive," noted Morris Silver.[54]

It was significantly earlier that complexity and bureaucratization of the political economy rendered sophisticated accounting systems necessary. Piotr Steinkeller found that the taxation system alone "called for an extraordinarily high level of data-recording."[55] At base it was the scale of production that called forth standardization, efficiency principles, bookkeeping procedures, and other innovations that we wrongly tend to think of as recent developments. Modern "firm-like" approaches are indeed thousands of years old.

The production of bronze required long-distance trade, and commonly involved copper shipments of many tons each. Excavations at Yarim Tepe revealed copper and lead smelting from about 6000 B.C., a surprisingly early date and a "hitherto unsuspected level of industrial specialization."[56] Ceramic production changed with the emergence of urbanism; pottery was increasingly wheel-made and uniform. As Childe put it, "with the adoption of the wheel, pottery tends to become a factory product and to lose much of its individuality."[57] The manufacture of glass vessels spread across the Near East upon its invention in the second millennium B.C. Textile enterprises had already reached enormous proportions. Around 2200 B.C., a weaving factory in Guabba employed over 6,000 workers, mostly women and children.[58]

Industrialism is a control apparatus by its nature, integrative in a primary sense. Mesopotamian writing, the world's earliest, is another example of a technology that arose to meet organizational requirements of the manufacturing economy. Writing made effective management of mass enterprises possible for the first time.

Thousands of years before twentieth-century Taylorists or Stakhovanite managers applied stopwatches to workers' motions in the U.S. and USSR, such practices were common in Mesopotamia. Soon after the hour was first divided into sixty minutes there, time became a weapon of mass production labor-discipline. "Ur III [late third millennium] timekeepers were extraordinarily punctilious in reckoning precisely how long it took to make ceramic vessels of varying size."[59] In other areas beside pottery fabrication, authorities "made constant efforts to standardize and rationalize."[60]

At this time a uniform model of beveled-rim bowls became ubiquitous. It now seems that they mainly served to provide standard wage rations (e.g. barley, oil), a very widespread usage.[61] It was a common practice for workers to borrow against wages in advance of payday, and "despite the growing emphasis on labor-saving products, techniques and organization, many people's workloads probably continued to increase," concluded Oppenheim.[62] So much of this has the ring of contemporaneity to it.

Trade union activity was widespread in the Middle Bronze Age, with unionization at far higher levels than in the U.S. today.[63] The risk of social unrest prompted "make-work" projects, such as elaborate public construction efforts[64]—more practices and sensibilities that seem distinctly modern.

Some of the people who weren't interested in civilization, or its regimen of work and cities, now were compelled to work as slaves. Debt slavery came later, but slave status was a generally fluid condition, marginal to society as a whole.[65]

Deforestation, grazing, and the extensive irrigation system created increasingly grave environmental impacts in Mesopotamia by the late third millennium. It was the last factor, unnatural amounts of water applied to the land, that may have been the most harmful. Irrigation brought up salt water through capillary action, creating wastelands and causing the abandonment of cities in the southern region.[66] The salinization effects were also felt in the Harappan civilization of India at this time (circa 2200 B.C.), and indeed are very problematic today, notably in Turkey, Australia, and Montana.[67]

By this same period, a wholesale-retail network of large-scale commodity exchange was in effect, providing the background to much that we would find familiar: commercial streets, taverns, broad avenues, plazas, alleys, empty lots, large and small houses—built of mud brick, plaster and wood, as in Iraq today. Neighborhood bakeries (likely the first shops), a very developed cuisine with a wide array of recipes (including farmed fish), sports, popular music, the first zoos, parks—many features that "must have made Mesopotamian cities vibrant, noisy, smelly, sometimes bewildering and dangerous, but also exciting places."[68] And in private life, all that survives today, from cosmetics and perfume to board games and tablecloths.

Urban Mesopotamia was virtually designed for epidemic disease, created by domestication and its first, Neolithic crowding of animals (human and otherwise), and perfected by city conditions. Another civilizational staple we have not left behind. Perhaps surprisingly, general longevity for adults was much the same as it is today.[69] Probably more unusual to us is the absence of racial divisions. For H.W.F. Saggs, it is "very clear" that "ethnic divisions played little part" in Mesopotamian society.[70] Upward mobility for the individual, then as now, was most common in periods of geographic or economic expansion.[71] There were women in business and the professions—far more so than in the Near East now—but they did not enjoy complete equality in law or custom.[72]

Mesopotamian complex society, for example the Uruk city-states, needed the resources of the Anatolian and Iranian highlands; they therefore tended toward expansion and war. Interference with trade routes, real or potentially real, could not be tolerated. The very recent wars in this same land demonstrate the same principle urging warfare, in the matter of guaranteed oil supply, of course.

Sargon (circa 2310 B.C.) was the first historical personality. He was the first ruler to establish a unified rule over all of Mesopotamia; in fact, his was the first world system polity. Sargon's triumph, amid growing degrees of warfare and imperialism, was not without challenges. Like most rulers he faced revolts, and agriculture as an institution met with persistent resistance.[73] Sargon II referred to the hill-country Mannaeans as living "in confusion," whom he had to civilize or "put into order."[74] A crescendo of aggression and warfare led to the crisis of twelfth-century Mesopotamia, three centuries of decline and collapse that represented the end of the Bronze Age.

Egypt, like Mesopotamia, was a new chapter or project of domestication. It became a civilizational answer to the uncertainty that those in power had to contend with when the Neolithic era ended. "Irrigation agriculture was decisive in generating civilization, stratification, and the state in Egypt," the Nile supporting "the highest population density" in the ancient world.[75] Lacking some of the strong early urban development seen in Mesopotamia, Egypt was—and remains—a mainly agricultural country. Its civilization rested on the surplus created in the fields; Robert July estimated that the average Egyptian peasant produced three times as much food as he needed.[76]

By about 3000 B.C. Egypt's chiefdoms and proto-states had been forged into the region's first nation-state, with a "sophisticated populace."[77] Lynn Meskell advises us that "we have underestimated the complexities of ancient cultures—Egypt being one of the most important."[78]

Sergio Donadoni observes that "the Egyptian world appears to be strikingly modern in many ways."[79]

Egyptian rulers, like those of Mesopotamia, claimed a genealogy going back to the gods. Nevertheless, it was the pharaoh's earthly power that was employed to subordinate "Egypt's own potentially rebellious population."[80] We know a lot less about how that population lived than we do about tombs and pyramids, largely because unlike cities and towns, non-urban artifacts were not repeatedly replaced and built over. Concerning the breadth and depth of religious feeling, for example, we can only really guess, although as today, various people might have looked forward to an afterlife that was a considerable improvement on the earthly one. The Egyptians were the first to embalm bodies, and the practice remained popular despite widespread tomb-robbing in ancient times. "During certain epochs," observed Donadoni, "it is quite likely that entire populations made a living out of the business."[81] This phenomenon would seem to undermine the notion of strong Egyptian piety. "There is some doubt," adds A.G. McDowell, "whether the common man was much concerned with what went on behind the temple pylons."[82]

It does seem clear that Egyptians favored local gods, which may be related to the common attitude that all animals were sacred.[83] In the end, however, the spiritual culture descended into a "religion-haunted, superstitious, ritualistic" condition.[84]

Egypt was essentially an exchange economy. The presence of components such as "wage-labor, a market for land, production for the market, and state involvement"[85] certainly qualified it as capitalist. Although Egypt has been described as a public sector economy,[86] Lynn Meskell's study of Deir el-Medina, the most thoroughly documented settlement site of Middle Kingdom Egypt, provides a more nuanced view. Meskell finds that "all the evidence points to a minimum interventionist model" where individuals "exercised a remarkable amount of social mobility and maneuvering, ignoring the sanctions of the state to their own personal benefit and profit."[87]

There were many, however, who worked directly for the state (e.g. bureaucrats, craftsmen), just as there are in any modern nation. Scribes became an intellectual class and staffed a functioning and growing bureaucracy. Many hoped to avoid manual labor by building an administrative career in the civil service. Over time a large number of immigrants, chiefly Asians, engaged in building and industrial activity.[88]

Some of the world's oldest underground mining activity took place in Egypt (e.g. Nazlet Khater-4). By the time of the New Kingdom in the late Bronze Age there was mass production of goods in several sectors. Marked craft specialization existed in metallurgy, lithic industry, stone vase production, and above all, pottery manufacturing.[89] Potters used an assembly-line mode "remarkably" early, in the judgment of Lionel Casson.[90] Increasing sameness was the rule, as quantity replaced distinctive quality as a value. Industrial vessels predominate over household pots in the archaeological record,[91] as befits a mass society.

Beer, bread, and wine were some of the production staples, plus an excellent form of paper that was widely exported. (The word derives from papyrus, the Egyptian reed from which paper was first made.) Late Egypt saw a number of sizeable textile factories.[92] The kingdom had arrived at "an unrivalled celebrity as a manufacturing country."[93] Pyramid building was a socio-economic enterprise, more focused on employment-based loyalty than motivated by religious ideology.[94] In any case, such monumentalism created an enormous demand for Lebanese cedar and pine, part of the major deforestation in the region.[95]

Egypt's chief contemporary archaeologist disclosed evidence in 2010 that the Great Pyramids were built by free workers, not by slaves.[96] This furthers the thesis that such projects had become economic necessities,[97] and that slavery was in general uneconomic and comparatively rare.[98] As in Mesopotamia, the institution had very different forms and meanings from our own definition. "Slave" was not a legal term; citizens and slaves were the same under the law, for example.[99]

In the world of work, one can pass from celebrated design perfection (e.g. tombs) and magnificent stone vessel craftsmanship to the dangerous drudgery in the mines (in any age or epoch), and the fact that scribes were as numerous as office workers are now.[100]

Workers were generally well paid in regular wages of grain, fish, vegetables, and the like, with bonus payments not uncommon.[101] Deir el-Medina laborers "were receiving good wages even when they were not needed."[102] Eyre found "no evidence that the wage levels of the crew were ever reduced, either individually or collectively, because of absences from work."[103]

The prominence of writing is clear at Deir el-Medina, and "some workmen read Middle Egyptian classics for pleasure and not merely for training."[104] The degree of proletarian literacy and culture in ancient Egypt is a surprising fact.[105]

Workers were fairly mobile, and in the case of unsolicited transfers were commonly displeased, much as in today's world. But legal agreements (and lawsuits) were far from rare, and neither were agreements that were explicitly labor contracts, it seems.[106] Skilled craftsmen and foremen often came up from the ranks,[107] and Marfoe noted an "emphasis on 'self-made' men and personal initiative [which is] a striking parallelism with the ethical changes and transformations of a later capitalistic age."[108]

Despite whatever upwardly mobile consciousness there may have been, class struggle was definitely present, especially toward the end of the Bronze Age. Strikes broke out during the reigns of Ramses III and IV in the twelfth and eleventh centuries B.C., often over late wages. The strikes of 1160–1153 B.C. are thought to be the first in history.[109] At times even the pharaoh couldn't get them back to work![110] Other heightened conflicts involved actions such as torch-lit night demonstrations and other forms of militant political activity "of a type more familiar from our own time."[111]

Ancient Egypt was somewhat less city-oriented than Mesopotamia, but did have towns and cities of considerable density.[112] Among their courtyards and byways, bars and suburbs, both opportunity and crime were present.[113] At least some municipalities had elaborate sewer systems for waste disposal and state-provided laundry services.[114] Meskell referred to evidence concerning urban masses "suggesting a richer material life than previously thought."[115] Casson tells us that despite the tombs, mummies, and grave art, Egyptians reveled in the refinement of living and "were a worldly, materialistic people."[116] There was also a relative simplicity: not a lot of property that needed guarding, and structures that were easily replaced in case of storms, flooding, or fire.[117] A lesson for us, especially in our age of worsening, volatile weather.

Much activity and social life took place at the roof level, as today in Egypt. Senet (Egyptian checkers) was played on a board of thirty squares. An Old Kingdom relief displays nineteen kinds of bread. The domestic cat makes its appearance at about 2100 B.C. Many people wore almost nothing during the hot summers, using straws to sip drinks bought at booths, cooled with ice from the mountains. The siesta was observed, and of course survives in some countries. It may be telling that a key issue in a strike of Thebes necropolis workers around 1170 B.C. was that their ration of ointment oil had not been provided.

A literature of romantic love, just as nuanced and complex as found in the West many, many centuries later, was part of the culture.[118] Along with the growth of literacy, "school education is perhaps the best known aspect of growing up in Ancient Egypt," paralleling the high regard for white-collar scribal professions.[119] "One surprising fact about life…is the amount of letter-writing,"[120] the extent to which persons of "fairly ordinary status" corresponded.[121]

Intellectuals gravitated toward the larger cities,[122] a tendency familiar to us. Tourism within Egypt was a popular pursuit.[123] By the late Bronze Age, festivals, celebrations, and entertainments were increasingly staged, and sports figures became glorified.[124] Justice was sought from the legal system and occasionally found, at least on the local level where juries were made up of average citizens.[125] Internalization of bureaucratic values was fairly widespread, as seen in career manuals that counseled a conformist, "quiet man" approach to success.[126]

Women could own property, run businesses, become doctors, but did not have the same rights as men.[127] Various roles were open to them, but their status was unequal, their position much more dependent on the standing of their spouses.[128] Divorce was fairly common, and same-sex relations—between men, at least—were accorded "a significant place in Middle Kingdom literature."[129] Love relationships, including marriage, could be fluid and complicated, causing the Janssens to observe that "perhaps in this respect Pharaonic Egypt most resembles our own days."[130]

At the end of the era the Greek Herodotus made note of the freedoms of Egyptian women: "in their manners and customs the Egyptians seem to have reversed the ordinary practices of mankind. For instance, women go to market and engage in trade, while men stay home and do the weaving."[131] A little later still, Philon was even more shocked: "As things are now, some women have reached such a degree of shamelessness that they not only, though they are women, give vent to intemperate language and abuse among a crowd of men, but even strike men and insult them…."[132] These comments may say more about their authors than about the position of women in Egypt, but Erika Feucht is on solid ground in concluding that their standing was "stronger than that of their modern sisters."[133]

From the Bronze Age as a whole, we have most of our present-day craft or hand tools, including hammers, chisels, drills, etc. Also pails, wire, safety pins, tweezers, razors, and many other common implements. The pervasive consumer culture practice of branding was begun in the fourth millennium, to boost sales.[134] There was a surprising amount of metalwork left on the ground, and thus wasted, in Bronze Age locales,[135] which could remind us that our throwaway practices are nothing new. Notions of Utopia first arose in this epoch,[136] likely evidence of movement away from what might be desired in society.

Egypt, after a long, relatively inward-looking orientation, created one of the world's earliest empires. By dominating Syro-Palestine and Nubia it temporarily achieved economic advances and overcame challenges to social order. But militarism only postponed the breakdown of political authority, exacerbated by major environmental destruction. The land surrounding the Nile, for example, had been turned into barren desert by overgrazing and deforestation.[137]

There had been a very significant crisis earlier (from circa 2150 B.C.), a so-called Dark Age that resulted in political fragmentation. Every form of looting, riot and revolution had broken forth, shattering the façade of royal security.[138] But the final breakdown, delayed by imperial adventure, came in about 1200 B.C. and brought an end to all Near East Bronze Age civilizations. A rather sudden and definitive collapse. The late Bronze Age, with its industrial progress, was a time of social turmoil and chronic war,[139] now the universal mark of civilization. The project of control and integration failed, as nomadic groups grew in prominence and palaces fell.

A "dramatic reorganization"[140] was urgently needed, and the new Iron Age arose to establish more efficient systems of power and dependence. World ("Axial") religions responded to those disoriented by the hollowness of civilization's achievements.[141] Monotheism, religion's next phase, was part of the turning-point rescue mission at a time of disintegration. Freud blamed Akhenaten for monotheism, but the Egyptian had failed to establish it in his own culture.

"Should we be surprised to learn that the first truly large societies had to be assembled by force, and eventually broke apart?" asks Kent Flannery.[142] Early civilizations, Mesopotamia and Egypt included, were "characterized by resistance to state power and therefore by instability and periodic breakdown."[143]

We are still in the Iron Age, civilization's current pacification effort, in the techno-industrial era of that age. Collapse has to be understood as an aspect or consequence of development itself, especially when the movement of civilization has meant more work, greater discipline, more elaborate social hierarchies, and greater economic inequality, not to mention grave psychic dislocation and impoverishment, and the destruction of nature.

Early civilizations exhibit many features that we encounter today, and one could see mass society already present in Bronze Age societies. The project of control and integration is unremitting, and as we have seen, it is not always successful. Worlds that are complex and unsatisfactory require constant legitimation and re-legitimation, evolving approaches and institutions.

As Mumford put it, "The sudden evaporation of meaning and value in a civilization, often at the moment when it seems at its height, has long been one of the enigmas of history."[144] Civilization today—a single, universal reality, its fearful toll terribly evident —is far from its "height." An opportunity to end it lies before us.

(ENDNOTES)

1 ¹ Jacques Cauvin, *The Birth of the Gods and the Origins of Agriculture*, translated by Trevor Watkins (New York: Cambridge University Press, 2000), p. 205.

2 Ian Kuit, "People and Space in Early Agricultural Villages: Exploring Daily Lives, Community, Size and Archaeology in the Late Pre-Pottery Neolithic," in *Journal of Anthropological Archaeology* 19 (March 2000), pp. 96–99.

3 John Baines, "Public Ceremonial Performance in Ancient Egypt," in Takeshi Inomata and Lawrence S. Cohen, eds., *Archaeology of Performance* (Lanham, MD: AltaMira Press, 2006), p. 263.

4 Bruce G. Trigger, *Understanding Early Civilizations: A Comparative Study* (New York: Cambridge University Press, 2003), p. 673.

5 John Baines, "Public Ceremonial Performance in Ancient Egypt," in Takeshi Inomata and Lawrence S. Cohen, eds., *Archaeology of Performance* (Lanham, MD: AltaMira Press, 2006), p. 263.

6 Stanley Diamond, *In Search of the Primitive: A Critique of Civilization* (New Brunswick, NJ: Transaction Books, 1974), pp. 4, 3.

7 Graeme Baker, "The Conditions of Cultural and Economic Growth in the Bronze Age of Central Italy," in *Proceedings of the Prehistoric Society* (1972), p. 204.

8 Oystein S. La Bianca, Introduction, in Oystein LaBianca and Sandra Arnold Scham, eds., *Connectivity in Antiquity* (London: Equinox, 2006), p. 7.

9 Sam Lilley, *Men, Machines and History* (London: Cobbett Press, 1948), p. 8.

10 Herbert J. Muller, *Freedom in the Ancient World* (New York: Harper & Brothers, 1961), p. 25.

11 V. Gordon Childe, *The Bronze Age* (New York: Cambridge University Press, 1930), p. 3.

12 Theodore A. Wertime, "The Furnace versus the Goat? Pyrotechnic Industries and Mediterranean Deforestation," *Journal of Field Archaeology* 10 (1983), pp. 445–452.

13 Trigger, *op.cit.*, p. 48.

14 Elman Service, *Origins of the State and Civilization* (New York: Norton, 1975), p. 223.

15 Monica L. Smith, *The Social Construction of Ancient Cities* (Washington, DC: Smithsonian Books, 2003), p. 28.

16 Vicente Lull and Rafael Nico, translated by Peter Smith, *Archaeology of the Origin of the State* (New York: Oxford University Press, 2011), p. 184.

17 Trigger, *op.cit.,* p. 52. There is some controversy as to whether a few large Neolithic settlements, such as Jericho and especially, Catul Huyuk (in present-day Turkey) constituted cities.

18 Cited in A. Mederos and C.C. Lamberg-Karlovsky, "Weight Systems and Trade Networks," in Jeremy A. Subloff and C.C. Lamberg-Karlovsky, eds., *Ancient Civilization and Trade* (Albuquerque: University of New Mexico Press, 1975), p. 207.

19 James Mellaart, *The Chalcolithic and Early Bronze Ages in the Near East and Anatolia* (Beirut: Khayats, 1966), p. 59.

20 Quoted from Martin Heidegger, "Why Do I Stay in the Provinces?" in Thomas Sheehan, ed., *Heidegger: The Man and the Thinker* (Chicago: Precedent Publishing, 1981), p. 29.

21 Marvin Harris, *Cultural Materialism* (New York: Random House, 1979), p. 100.

22 Trigger, *op.cit.,* p. 196.

23 Richard Sennett, *Flesh and Stone: The Body and the City in Western Civilization* (New York: W.W. Norton, 1994), p. 106.

24 Michael Mann, *The Sources of Social Power, Volume I: A History of Power from the Beginning to A.D. 1760* (New York: Cambridge University Press, 1986), p. 48.

25 Muller, *op.cit.,* p. 27.

26 Kristian Kristiansen, *Europe Before History* (New York: Cambridge University Press, 1998), pp 133, 411.

27 Justin Jennings, *Globalizations and the Ancient World* (New York: Cambridge University Press, 2011), p. 17.

28 Andre Gunder Frank and Barry K. Gills, *The World System: Five Hundred Years or Five Thousand?* (New York: Routledge, 1993), p. 1.

29 Kasja Ekholm Friedman and Jonathan Friedman, *Historical Transformations: The Anthropology of Global Systems* (Lanham, MD: AltaMira Press, 2008), p. 163.

30 Quoted in Frank and Gills, *op.cit.,* p. 13.

31 Andrew and Susan Sherratt, cited in Frank and Gills, *op.cit.,* p. 21.

32 A. Leo Oppenheim, *Ancient Mesopotamia: Portrait of a Dead Civilization* (Chicago: University of Chicago Press, 1977), p. 111.

33 Burt Alpert, *Inversions* (San Francisco: privately published, 1973), p. 294.

34 Louis L. Orlin, *Life and Thought in the Ancient Near East* (Ann Arbor: University of Michigan Press, 2007), p. 162.

35 Jennings, *op.cit.,* p. 76.

36 J.N. Postgate, *Early Mesopotamia: Society and Economy at the Dawn of History* (New York: Routledge, 1992), p. 225.

37 Robert McC. Adams, "Patterns of Urbanism in Early Southern Mesopotamia," in Peter J. Ucko, Ruth Tringham, and G.W. Dimberly, eds., *Man, Settlement and Urbanism* (London: Duckworth, 1972), p. 745.

38 Jonathan Haas, ed., *From Leaders to Rulers* (New York: Kluwer Academic/Plenum Publishers, 2001), p. 218. And Oppenheim, *op.cit.,* p. 72.

39 Robin Winks and Susan P. Mattern-Parkes, *The Ancient Mediterranean World* (New York: Oxford University Press, 2004), p. 24.

40 Orlin, *op.cit.,* pp 172–173.

41   Peter Machinist, "On Self-Consciousness in Mesopotamia," in S.N. Eisenstadt, *The Origins and Diversity of Axial Age Civilizations* (Albany: State University of New York Press, 1986), p. 187.

42   Oppenheim, *op.cit.*, p. 109.

43   Cited in Karen Rhea Nemet-Nejat, Daily Life in Ancient Mesopotamia (Peabody, MA: Hendrickson Publishers, 2002), p. 107.

44   Oppenheim, *op.cit.*, p. 191.

45   David and Joan Oates, *The Rise of Civilization* (New York: Elsevier Phaidon, 1976), p. 134.

46   *Ibid.*, p. 135.

47   Trigger, *op.cit.*, p. 219.

48   Nemet-Nejat, *op.cit.*, p. 302. Postgate, *op.cit.*, p. 300.

49   Lewis Mumford, *The City in History* (New York: Harcourt, Brace & World, 1961), p. 53.

50   Oates and Oates, *op.cit.*, p. 67.

51   Norman Yoffee, "Mesopotamian Interaction Spheres," in Norman Yoffee and Jeffery J. Clark, *Early Stages in the Evolution of Mesopotamian Civilization* (Tucson: University of Arizona Press, 1993), p. 267.

52   Charles Keith Maisels, *Early Civilizations of the Old World* (New York: Routledge, 1999), p. 346.

53   Morris Silver, *Economic Structures of Antiquity* (Westport, CT: Greenwood Press, 1995), pp. 154, 156.

54   *Ibid.*, p. 114.

55   Quoted in Introduction, Michael Hudson and Cornelia Wunsch, eds., *Creating Economic Order* (Bethesda, MD: CDL Press, 2004), p. 9.

56   Oates and Oates, *op.cit.*, p. 101.

57   Childe, *op.cit.*, p. 51. Also P.R.S. Moorey, *Ancient Mesopotamian Materials and Industries* (Oxford: Clarendon Press, 1994), p. 157.

58   Postgate, *op.cit.*, p. 235.

59   D.T. Potts, *Mesopotamian Civilization: The Material Foundations* (Ithaca, NY: Cornell University Press, 1997), p. 156.

60   Postgate, *op.cit.*, p. 233.

61   Oates and Oates, *op.cit.*, p. 130.

62   Oppenheim, *op.cit.*, p. 96.

63   Alpert, *op.cit.*, pp 296–298.

64   Oppenheim, *op.cit.*, p. 98.

65   Nemet-Nejat, *op.cit.*, pp 117–118.

66   Postgate, *op.cit.*, p. 181.

67   Jared Diamond, *Collapse* (New York: Viking, 2005), p. 48.

68   Susan Pollock, *Ancient Mesopotamia: The Eden That Never Was* (New York: Cambridge University Press, 1999), p. 48.

69   Nemet-Nejat, *op.cit.*, p. 146.

70   H.W.F. Saggs, *Civilization Before Greece and Rome* (New Haven: Yale University Press, 1989), p. 45.

71   Trigger, *op.cit.*, p. 161.

72   Postgate, *op.cit.*, p. 105.

73   Service, *op.cit.*, p. 215.

74   Machinist/Eisenstadt, *op.cit.*, p. 189.

75   Mann, *op.cit.*, p. 108.

76   Robert W. July, *A History of the African People* (New York: Scribner, 1970), p. 14.

77 Lionel Casson, *Everyday Life in Ancient Egypt* (Baltimore: Johns Hopkins University Press, 2001), p. 1.

78 Lynn Meskell, *Archaeologies of Social Life: Age, Sex, Class et cetera in Ancient Egypt* (Malden, MA: Blackwell, 1999), p. 110.

79 Sergio Donadini, ed., *The Egyptians* (Chicago: The University of Chicago Press, 1997), p. x.

80 Edith Lustig, "Anthropology and Egyptology," in A. Bernard Knapp, ed., *Monographs in Mediterranean Archaeology* 8 (Sheffield, UK: Sheffield Academic Press, 1997), p. 14.

81 Sergio Donadini, "The Dead," in Donadini, *op.cit.*, p. 272.

82 A.G. McDowell, *Village Life in Ancient Egypt* (New York: Oxford University Press, 1990), p. 91. Also, "The tomb of Tutankhamen was partially looted by the very priests responsible for the burial" (p. 199). And "By 1064 B.C. at the latest it was patently clear that all the major royal tombs in the Valley of the Kings had been looted" (p. 242).

83 Casson, *op.cit.*, pp 89, 83.

84 *Ibid.*, p. 120.

85 David Warburton, *State and Economy in Ancient Egypt* (Freiburg, Switzerland: University Press, 1997), p. 173.

86 Eric Carlton, *Ideology and Social Order* (Boston: Routledge & Kegan Paul), p. 134.

87 Lynn Meskell, *Private Life in New Kingdom Egypt* (Princeton: Princeton University Press, 2002), p. 25.

88 Gae Callender, "The Middle Kingdom Renaissance," in *The Oxford History of Ancient Egypt* (New York: Oxford University Press, 2003), p. 157.

89 Casson, *op.cit.*, p. 53.

90 *Ibid.*, p. 54.

91 Max Raphael, *Prehistoric Pottery and Civilization in Egypt* (New York: Pantheon Books, 1947), p. 135.

92 Naphtali Lewis, *Life in Egypt Under Roman Rule* (Oxford: Clarendon Press, 1983), p. 134.

93 J. Gardner Wilkinson, *Manners and Customs of the Ancient Egyptians* (London: John Murray, 1841), p. 4.

94 Carlton, *op.cit.*, p. 139. The Aztec state was another that consolidated power through large-scale public works projects.

95 Mellaart, *op.cit.*, p. 68.

96 Marwa Awad, "Egypt Tombs Suggest Pyramids not Built by Slaves," Thomson Reuters, January 10, 2010.

97 Kurt Mendelssohn, "A Scientist Looks at the Pyramids," in *American Scientist* 59:2 (1971), pp. 210-220. After about 2600 B.C. some thirty-five major pyramids and many smaller ones were built, along with large monuments such as Abu Simbel. Architecture and art of this kind are ultimately about governance as well as economics. A sense of power and order is transmitted, as is the case with contemporary examples (e.g. Washington Monument).

98 Shaw, *op.cit.*, p. 421.

99 Antonio Loprieno, "Slaves," in Donadini, *op.cit.*, pp 206-216. Also Edward Eyre, "Work in the New Kingdom," in Marvin A. Powell, ed., *Labor in the Ancient Near East* (New Haven: American Oriental Society, 1987), p. 211.

100 Casson, *op.cit.*, p. 50.

101 McDowell, *op.cit.*, pp. 7, 223. And Rosalind M. and Jac J. Janssen, *Growing Up in Ancient Egypt* (London: The Rubicon Press, 1990), p. 107.

102 *Ibid.*, p. 80.

103 Edward Eyre in Powell, *op.cit.*, p. 178.

104 McDowell, *op.cit.*, p. 137.

105 Janssen and Janssen, *op.cit.*, p. 86.

106 Jill Kamil, *The Ancient Egyptians: Life in the Old Kingdom* (Cairo: The American University in Cairo Press, 1996), p. 169.

107 Dominique Valbelle, "Craftsmen," in Donadini, *op.cit.*, p. 48.

108 Leon Marfoe, "Early Near Eastern Societies," in Michael J. Rowlands, Mogen Larsen, Kristian Kristiansen, eds., *Centre and Periphery in the Ancient World* (Cambridge: Cambridge University Press, 1986), pp. 27–28.

109 Shaw, *op.cit.*, p. 298. And Casson, *op.cit.*, p. 80.

110 John Romer, *People of the Nile* (New York: Crown Publishers, 1982), p. 195.

111 Robyn Gillam, *Performance and Drama in Ancient Egypt* (London: Duckworth, 2005), p. 92.

112 T.G.H. James, *Pharaoh's People: Scenes from Life in Imperial Egypt* (Chicago: The University of Chicago Press, 1984), p. 215.

113 Meskell 2002, *op.cit.*, p. 34.

114 Saggs, *op.cit.*, p. 122. McDowell, *op.cit.*, p. 59.

115 Meskell 2002, *op.cit.*, p. 36.

116 Casson, *op.cit.*, p. 145. Barbara Mertz, *Red Land, Black Land: The World of the Ancient Egyptians* (New York: Coward-McCann, 1966), p. 298.

117 Gaston C.C. Maspero, *Life in Ancient Egypt and Assyria* (New York: Frederick Ungar, 1971 [1892]), pp. 2–5.

118 Meskell 2002, *op.cit.*, p. 127.

119 Janssen and Janssen, *op.cit.*, p. 89.

120 Mertz, *op.cit.*, p. 142.

121 James, *op.cit.*, p. 165.

122 Carlton, *op.cit.*, p. 105.

123 Mertz, *op.cit.*, p. 129.

124 John A. Wilson, *The Culture of Ancient Egypt* (Chicago: The University of Chicago Press, 1968), p. 195.

125 James, *op.cit.*, p. 88.

126 Trigger, *op.cit.*, pp 627, 635.

127 Erika Feucht, "Women," in Donadini, *op.cit.*, p. 344.

128 Meskell 2002, *op.cit.*, p. 56.

129 *Ibid.*, p. 145.

130 Janssen and Janssen, *op.cit.*, p. 113.

131 Herodotus, *History* II.35, Quoted in Sennett, *op.cit.*, p. 381.

132 Quoted in Jack Lindsay, *Leisure and Pleasure in Roman Egypt* (New York: Barnes & Noble, 1966), p. 346.

133 Feucht/Donadini, *op.cit.*, p. 346.

134 David Wengrow, "Prehistories of Commodity Branding," *Current Anthropology* 49:1 (2008), pp. 7-34.

135 A.F. Harding, *European Societies in the Bronze Age* (New York: Cambridge University Press, 2000), p. 352.

136 Jack Goody, *Food and Love: A Cultural History of East and West* (New York: Verso, 1998), p. 242.

137 Donald J. Ortner, *How Humans Adapt: A Biocultural Odyssey* (Washington, DC: Smithsonian Institution Press, 1983), p. 202.

138 Carlton, *op.cit.*, p. 67.

139 Childe, *op.cit.*, pp. 192–193.

140 A. Sestiari, A. Cazzella, and A. Schlapp, "The Mediterranean," in Barry Cunliffe, Wendy Davis, and Colin Renfrew, eds., *Archaeology: The Widening Debate* (Oxford: Oxford University Press, 2002), p. 427.

141 Mumford, *op.cit.*, p. 77. See John Zerzan, "The Iron Grip of Civilization: The Axial Age," in my *Twilight of the Machines* (Port Townsend, WA: Feral House, 2008), pp. 27–37.

142 Kent V. Flannery, "Process and Agency in Early State Formation," *Cambridge Archaeological Journal* 9:1 (April 1999), p. 18.

143 Trigger, *op.cit.*, p. 27.

144 Mumford, *op.cit.*, p. 69.

Arrivederci Roma: The Crisis of Late Antiquity

Edward Gibbon wrote *The History of the Decline and Fall of the Roman Empire* in the 1780s, and it remains a classic. Beyond the merits and deficiencies of his Enlightenment creation stands its title, in itself an enduring proposition. That is, many have wondered whether their own time and place—especially in recent times—is not also experiencing a decline and fall. Today, for example, do we not see a parallel to "the spiritual and social exhaustion of the Roman world"[1]?

Getting back to the subject, it was more than just the Empire that declined and fell. Rome's authority melted away in the fifth and sixth centuries A.D. And Greco-Roman civilization itself disintegrated and vanished—socially, culturally, politically, and militarily. It was a rupture unparalleled in the history of the West.

There are some who deny this, seeing, rather, only a bit of transition or adjustment. Noel Lenski, for instance: "The model of decline and fall is…a modern invention, which we have finally begun to cast off in our postmodern world."[2] Just as postmodernism "casts off" change in general, or the possibility of change.

More intelligently, Aldo Schiavone—and to some degree, Michael Rostovtzeff and F.W. Walbank before him—asks a very probing question: why didn't Roman society, so fully developed a civilization, continue directly on to modernity rather than fail?[3] Why did it have to fall apart and require a new start?

A partly valid answer is the standard one, provided by Gibbon, among others. It was Rome's "immoderate greatness,"[4] with frontiers that ranged across all of Europe, North Africa, and the Levant. Rome could not persevere forever, faced with "barbarians" on every side. I will take up barbarians later, but note in passing a barbarian's remark recorded by Tacitus: "They [the Romans, of course] make a desert and call it peace."[5]

The Marxist explanation is that Greco-Roman civilization was based on slavery, and the transition toward a feudal system meant the end of that whole structure.

Rome was fully formed, a civilization of vast extent but insufficient depth. There had been a basis of traditional bonds and reciprocities underlying all else. It slowly broke down, socially and economically, and "unraveled down to its smallest elements between the sixth and seventh centuries."[6] A malaise settled over every sphere of life, beginning in the second century, deepening into exhaustion, sterility, and resignation. Learning was neglected, for example, with the gardens of Epicurus and the portico of the Stoics almost deserted.[7] Knowledge no longer mattered.

Some achievements did endure. Oswald Spengler argued that the last phase of any civilization is a technological one. Trajan's second-century 3,000-foot Danube Bridge comes to mind, along with aqueducts that are still standing, and public baths and latrines, the latter with heated marble seats![8]

Rome began as a small settlement on the Tiber, in the eighth century B.C. if not earlier. By 270 B.C. its power had been consolidated throughout Italy. And by this time, gold, silver, grain and slaves flowed into the Roman treasury from other conquests. When the new millennium arrived, however, "the people of the Empire were obsessed with a vague feeling of deterioration."[9] Well underway by 200 A.D. was a sharpening of class divisions and "the accumulation of wealth and status into ever fewer hands."[10]

At the same time that the wealth, including slaves, of far-flung regions began to run dry, it was clear that "everywhere the extension of Roman rule had elicited armed resistance."[11] Rome became increasingly dependent for its defense on barbarian warriors; there had been "virtually no Italians in the ranks of the legions since the time of Trajan" in the second century.[12] In fact, "by the late fourth century even slaves were sometimes enlisted."[13]

Rising dissatisfaction within a stagnating economy brought a period of unparalleled crisis between 235 and 284, "during which the Roman Empire nearly came to an end."[14] According to Rostovtzeff, this crisis was largely brought about by "a revolutionary movement of the masses of the population which aimed at a general leveling."[15] Rome weathered the storm, and in the process became an absolute monarchy. The long period of challenge transformed the defensive Empire into what had not heretofore been seen in this part of the world: an absolutist state. Rome had emerged from the crisis, but was much weakened.[16]

Compared with the third century, the fourth was a time of governmental stability and economic improvement. It was also, as Ramsay MacMullen put it, "the great age of tax collectors."[17] There was a reason why the early medieval hymn "Dies Irae" conceived of the Day of Judgment in terms of the arrival of the late Roman tax collector. The state began to impose intolerable burdens upon town and country: "heavier taxes and an oppressive system of forced services and requisitions."[18] At the same time, the currency was repeatedly debased (with less gold and silver in the coinage), and rural depopulation set in.

The end neared in the fifth century as a period of "stark and rapid economic decline, perhaps unprecedented in recorded human history,"[19] afflicted much of the Empire. Early on, North Africa fell to the Vandals, with a crippling loss of tax revenues from Rome's wealthiest province. Also compromised thereby was much of the grain and oil subsidies to the Roman populace, half of the well-known "bread and circuses." Gladiatorial contests had been a legacy of the early-conquered Etruscans, with widespread construction of coliseums for the "circuses" to entertain the urban masses. These were something of a priority, usually built before public baths.

A climate of futility and decay could not be dispelled by government, despite military decrees, enforced by many agents, spies, and informers, to monitor Roman subjects.[20] In the countryside, tenant farmers were now tied to the land along with their heirs, a significant move toward serfdom.

Rome itself was breached and sacked several times, the final blow falling in 476 when barbarian mercenaries deposed the last Western Roman emperor. Byzantium and its capital of Constantinople survived, the Eastern remnant of Greco-Roman civilization. In the same year of 529 Justinian closed the university of Athens, and Benedict founded the first monastery of the West on Monte Cassino. Not until 554 was Roman authority at last re-established in Italy.

A sense of decline had long been underway, along with a lurking fearfulness.[21] A basic part of the background for this, basic to civilization, is the erosion of community and the separation of the individual from communal bonds. The most primary driver of this process, and most primary to civilization, is division of labor. In Late Antiquity we see activities transformed into professions, e.g. legal specialists. Formal and informal dress codes developed to distinguish the various orders, and in portraiture there is less attention to individuality, "in order to focus on the insignia of a role, with laborious exactitude."[22]

The general poverty of intellectual life was a clear sign of decline, as it is today. Despite imperial support, higher studies of all types languished. Fewer schools existed, less was written and read, original thought was wanting. There was a dearth of handbooks, encyclopedias, maps, etc. According to Carlin Barton, there was "a positive hostility toward the life of the mind," dating from the 300s, possibly earlier.[23]

The universe became devoid of meaning and a stratum of irrationality thickened over Rome's final centuries. "The mass of the people, dispirited and depressed, found hope in magic and superstition or in ancient cults, Oriental mystery religions, and Christianity."[24]

Various forms of pervasive violence perhaps also forecast a failing system of domination. Painful obligations on the citizenry produced resistance and, in turn, extraordinarily punitive measures. Restraint on the part of the powerful was lost, even as the legal right of the individual to decent treatment was steadily degraded. Judicial punishment was "specially aggressive, harsh, and ruthless," really amounting to cruel savagery.[25]

The ruling classes, concluded Peter Brown, carried a "static electricity of violence."[26] At school future Church father Augustine encountered the violence of well-to-do students who called themselves the Wreckers.[27] By the fourth century Augustine's fellow bishops had taken notice of "the endemic domestic violence of the upper classes."[28] Nor was this confined to the elites. Philosopher and anatomist Galen's *On the Passions and Errors of the Soul* had much to say about violent outbursts, judging that "The passions have increased in the souls of the majority of men to such a point that they are incurable diseases."[29]

Besides the symptoms of internal emptiness and anxiety in a civilization waning in meaning, there were barbarians; and in the popular account it was their repeated invasions that proved fatal. Kenneth Clark put it this way: "By the year 1000…the long dominance of the barbarian wanderers was over, and Western Europe was prepared for its first great age of civilization."[30] That's us, of course.

They were "not particularly numerous," as E.T. Salmon remarks.[31] The Vandals, who conquered the richest province of the Empire, were "a small people…indisputably weak when measured against Rome," found David Lambert.[32] Many historians have seen the barbarians as more notable for their incorporation into the fabric of the West than for their invasions.[33] More often than not, they were enrolled in the Empire's defense, as the number of Italians available for the legions steadily declined.

Not that this was always a seamless proposition. The Goths, for example, made a substantial military contribution, but not as an integral part of Rome's armies. Their autonomy meant that their loyalty could be shaky. But even in Rome's worst of times, barbarians in general "regularly disclaimed any intention or desire of destroying it."[34] The Gothic chieftain Alaric sacked Rome in 410, disappointed in his desire to become a high Roman official.[35] He had already been a mercenary in the pay of both the Western and Byzantine parts of the Empire.

Sometimes loyal, sometimes untrustworthy, the "barbarian" as a figure served various ideological purposes. Violent barbarians were used to justify huge military expenditures by the state.[36] Portrayed as noble savages, they were a means of criticizing degenerate civilization. *On the Government of God* was Salvian's fifth-century Christian take on the virtuous simplicity of barbarians vs. debased Romans. Earlier and more famously, the historian Tacitus praised moral, democratic, hospitable, and happy denizens to the north in his *Treatise on the Situation, Manners and Inhabitants of Germany.*[37] Petrus Patricius described the Scythians, in the east, as having "jeered at those who were shut up in the cities, saying, 'They live a life not of men but of birds sitting in their nests aloft; they leave the earth which nourishes them and choose barren cities; they put their trust in lifeless things rather than in themselves.'"[38]

In modern times J.B. Bury referred to Slavonic barbarians of late Rome "who could defy the justice of civilization in thick forests and inaccessible ravines—regions echoing with the wild songs and romances of outlaw life."[39] But the "barbarians" in Europe had been practicing domestication for at least four millennia, and the processes of state formation had been going on for four hundred years in the Germanic world. Nonetheless not all the earlier, freer modes were extinguished. Bury again: "The east German barbarians were still in the stage in which steady habits of work seem repulsive and dishonorable."[40]

And though various tribes had versions of "a warrior-aristocracy far removed from the tastes and ambitions of their own rank and file,"[41] not to mention kings, they structured their authority very much after the Roman model.[42] Theodoric wrote the emperor in 508 to assert that "Our royalty is an imitation of yours, modeled on your own good purpose, a copy of the only Empire."[43] King of the Germanic Ostrogoths, his aim was to restore the glory of Rome.

Going back as far as fifth century B.C. Herodotus, one can find the warlike quality of barbarians seen as a result of contact with a succession of rapacious Mediterranean empires.[44] Far more recently, E.A. Thompson argued that slavery in the Germanic world was the exception and that it was only much developed "in the two areas where Roman influence was the most extreme" and civilization the most advanced.[45]

Aside from the nature of barbarian society and/or its dialectic with Rome—and the difficulty of generalizing about various groups—there were some connections with Romans that may seem surprising. Peter Sarris wrote of fourth-century Goths and their "campaign of destruction aimed at members of the Roman governing classes"—in which "the barbarians were expressly aided…by members of the Roman lower classes."[46] In *On the Government of God*, the Christian author Salvian declared, "A large part of Gaul and Spain is already Gothic, and all the Romans who live there have only one wish, not to become Romans again."[47] Joseph Tainter saw it similarly: "Contemporary records indicate that, more than once, both rich and poor wished that the barbarians would deliver them from the burdens of the Empire."[48]

The dominant idea remained that only those who dwelled in cities were civilized; Roman civilization promoted urbanization. This was not limited to the capital, but "the early years of the fourth century A.D. saw a great increase in the population of Rome."[49]

Oswald Spengler declared an endpoint to civilization to be the triumph of the inorganic world-city over the organic land. (See especially "The Soul of the City" in *The Decline of the West*, volume II.) The Marxist Kautsky, Spengler's opposite politically, also observed the loss of contact with nature and the unmooring of the individual from ancestral supports.[50] Excessive urbanization was the main cause of the Roman collapse, in the opinion of Guglielmo Ferrero.[51]

It was "a world of dwindling towns and bloated cities"[52] in which the countryside was taxed and exploited to sustain urban living, resulting in rural depopulation. Meanwhile the urban framework was itself falling apart. The mounting stresses on Roman civilization, its empire in retreat, meant a "hard" regime tending toward what we would call privatization. Less expenditure for public buildings and public cults. "The cities, which had created and sustained the higher forms of economic life, gradually decayed, and the majority of them practically disappeared from the face of the earth," to quote Rostovtzeff.[53]

"Mass unrest," often due to food shortages, was "an inevitable phenomenon in cities of the Roman world," in A.D. Lee's words.[54] Robert Knapp found that "the natural recourse was to riot."[55] There was substantial social war violence from the Middle Empire to the end of late antiquity.[56] The fourth-century soldier and historian Ammianus Marcellinus wrote of the prominence of violent unrest in Rome, blaming the ruling class for disturbances and squalor.[57] Significant riots include a 348 clash over delay of the grain subsidy and repeated incidents in 365 over the high price of wine.

Antioch saw major riots in the fifth century, and Peter Brown characterized Alexandria as "a notoriously riot-prone city,"[58] to cite just a couple of non-Rome locations. Solomon Katz mentioned "terrible peasant revolts" in various parts of the Empire,[59] while outlawry became an important presence.

Between the late third century and the first half of the fifth, the Bagaudae, described as both brigands and revolutionaries, embodied outlaw peasant rebellion in parts of Gaul and Spain. Their egalitarian risings against the rich were a powerful radical critique in action.[60]

What came to be referred to as paganism was a mainstay of Greco-Roman civilization. It was the official ensemble of gods and rites, emphasizing the citizen's responsibility to imperial authority, and embodying unity. In this way paganism was close to a general attitude of patriotism, respectful of civic tradition. Victor Ehrenberg declared paganism to be "a political rather than a religious matter...no question of belief or even emotional feeling."[61] Its ritualism left little room for spirit, its orientation more empirical than a matter of faith. And since its gods were tied to the reigning politics, paganism tended toward the same breakdown Rome was experiencing. Its gods belonged to an early age, and were far from omnipotent. Civilization renders citizens powerless, and its religious parallel is a monotheistic, unrivaled power over its subjects in the spiritual realm.

The word pagan originally meant one who lives in a *pagus*, or village. It didn't exist as a religious term before Christians began calling non-Christians pagans. But the usage is clear enough to us, and though it had about seven centuries of tradition behind it by the 400s, paganism was lacking in substance. Too impersonal and far from totalizing, this civic religion was unable to bear much weight. It was overdue for a crisis, along with the rest of the ruling order. The old gods were too limited and too formal. They fell into the shade.

Roman globalization acquainted people with other options, via travel, trade, and conquest. With increasing insecurity, a feeling of "cosmic pessimism" grew steadily stronger.[62] So-called "mystery religions" arrived, mainly from the East, as misery begot mysticism. Mithra worship became a mystery cult from a branch of Persian Mazdaism, via the Greeks. It was fairly strong in the army, but its appeal was limited by its exclusion of women. From Egypt arose sun worship, the cult of Sol Invictus with his December 25 birthday, and also an Isis cult. Dionysus emerged, a powerful, universalizing god of salvation, prefiguring the Christian savior in several respects.[63] Native paganism in its last stages took on a Neo-Platonic coloring, a decidedly monotheistic move like most of the other religious tendencies, but not decisively enough.

The emperor Constantine converted to Christianity in 312, made it Rome's official religion, and declared paganism illegal. Anti-pagan repression was often laxly pursued, however, and two centuries after Constantine the old cults lingered. Paganism persisted in part because of its lack of a center; still largely polytheistic, it was multiple and versatile.[64] But especially in its old Roman dress, paganism continued to fade in the sixth century, its sacrifices and temples abandoned.[65] By the 390s the Christian church, a unified institution, had already visibly secured its hegemony.[66]

Christianity had rather suddenly and unexpectedly succeeded, providing a personal religion in place of an impersonal civic one. "Seldom has a small minority played so successfully on the anxieties of society," as Peter Brown put it.[67] Its central and original message of love was preached to the poor, the burdened, the outcast, not excluding women and slaves. Christian populism caught on with many in Roman civilization, especially the miserable urban masses. It not only offered heavenly reward, but also a stronger sense of belonging than that of the devotees of Mithra or Isis, for example.[68]

Another central focus was of course Christian belief in a resurrected figure, Jesus as divine Savior. It is clear that the early Christians expected an impending return of Christ, which gave their efforts a special intensity. The unique status of women and Christian care for the sick during epidemics were more down-to-earth contributors to success. The original churches were homes, which in itself gave women prominence, but during the third century the status of women was beginning to decline.[69]

The Gospel of Luke, written in about 100, contains many condemnations of the rich, e.g. "It is easier for a camel to go through a needle's eye, than for a rich man to enter the kingdom of God" (18:24). These were typical radical sentiments—which became inconvenient as the Church grew to be a powerful financial institution by the end of the third century.[70] "The time was ripe for a reconciliation of state and church, each of which needed the other," in Rostovtzeff's judgment.[71] Early on there were Christians who appreciated the relation between one god and one state, the helpful implications of monotheism for a universal and unified civilization.[72] Constantine, less abstractly, came to the conclusion that Christianity was the only glue that could help hold conflicting social elements together. The old ruling elites, or paideia, were no longer able to maintain control. With Christianity as the new public religion, religious and secular authority became integrated in a more binding and powerful partnership.

Preaching in fourth-century Antioch, John Chrysostom proclaimed, "Oh! how passing wonderful is the power of Christianity, that it restrains and bridles a man...."[73] Ambrose of Milan, another Church father and an aristocrat, in the same vein in 388: "The bishops are the controllers of the crowds, the keen upholders of peace...."[74] He also asserted that "priests should have nothing of the masses about them, nothing of the people, nothing in common with the pursuits and manners of the barbarous multitude."[75]

Christians had made the poor visible, and soon enough this made them more amenable to control. The Church took over much of the state's almsgiving and adopted a new style of pacification in civilization's never-ending task of securing its authority. More or less always stated in religious terms, the power of bishops, with their scores of guards, could hardly develop otherwise than along lines in tandem with the secular economy and society.

Rather like "closed shop" employment, where expulsion from the union spells loss of that employment, excommunication had temporal as well as spiritual consequences. It enforced the temporal power; e.g. soldiers who refused to fight in a war that the Church deemed just faced excommunication. Bishops preached increasingly to the elites, and the papacy made more and more of Rome's glorious past. And yet Christianity never lost its power to offer a radical sense of community, even if that community was more symbolic than actual.

A monolithic and centrally organized religion and its professional hierarchy took charge of various administrative functions of the Christianized Empire,[76] including roles performed by barbarian authorities. The growing Church to some extent took over what Rome had created. Of course, there existed various philosophical differences; the searching criticisms of Augustine and—as we have seen—Salvian come to mind. A united front against common enemies of church and state certainly held sway, however. It is clear that almost every emperor urged the Church to define correct doctrine so as to enforce its official monopoly.[77] Intolerance in matters of dogma was a new arrival to the Mediterranean world. Doctrine is of supreme importance for the first time in civilization.

A striking counterpoint to the accommodationist, power-oriented direction of the Church was a primitivist monasticism that swept the Roman world in the 300s. It began in the deserts of Egypt, where the number of radically ascetic monks neared 200,000 by the beginning of the fourth century.[78] The impulse to return to a pre-Fall, Eden-like simplicity pitted the movement against the Church hierarchy, civic authority, urban life, and even culture itself.[79] Historians such as Rufinus described the ability of monks to mingle with wild animals. Their revolt favored egalitarian virtue over the achievements of civilization. "They had dropped out of the world, because they found society more than they could endure," concluded Michael Grant.[80] Bishops frequently allied with local elites to bar monks from their towns and to defend the ancient customs. "Emperors, too, in their edicts, declared the inmates of the monasteries to be fanatical, unruly, and rebellious."[81]

Violence was a not uncommon response to this challenge, which reached a high point with the Circumcellions in North Africa, in the second half of the fourth century. The anarchic offshoot of a non-radical sectarian heresy, Circumcellions (vagabonds, literally) sought to restore the primitive equality of humankind. These millennium-seekers attracted fugitive slaves and destitute peasants, and their base consisted of native Berber and Punic elements.[82] Hostile to urbanism and the dominant order, they preserved their independence until the Muslim conquests of the eighth century suppressed all forms of Christianity in the region.

Most historians have agreed that the end of late antiquity coincided with the end of slavery. Slaves in earlier civilizations tended to be few compared with those of Greco-Roman civilization.[83] In the latter era slavery was extended from the sphere of domestic labor to the mines, fields, and workshops, but it seems to have been fading in the late Empire. Walter Scheidel argues that the number of slaves in Italy was "significantly smaller than previously thought"[84] even before an overall decline set in.

Peter Sarris contends that "there is every sign that agricultural slavery continued to be a widespread reality in late antiquity,"[85] but the new, bigger estates moved away from slave labor, according to Niall McKeown.[86] There were few or no slave rebellions; the Spartacus revolt, for instance, occurred several centuries earlier. But slaves escaped in large numbers, a continuous feed for outlawry.[87] The Romans, as McKeown put it, citing other historians, were "having serious difficulties controlling their slaves."[88] There was movement toward their replacement by the "colonate"—those tied to the land, toward the serf condition of medieval times.

Another transition involved the symbolic institution or dimension of time. For the Greeks, cyclical time still held sway. Their sense of historical or linear time remained quite tentative at best. Roman Stoics (e.g. Cicero and Seneca) introduced a progressive, non-repetitive concept later developed further by Augustine. We have been under the sign of historical temporality ever since. Restlessly striving to dominate it somehow, while unable to escape the helplessness resulting from civilized, complex society.

Rome's thousand years were, at base, just another civilization that came and went, subject once again to longings and anxious disquiet and requiring yet another new model of the same. Carlin Barton, in her often brilliant *Sorrows of the Ancient Romans*, refers to the Roman confrontation with time: "They were terrified by beginnings; this dread was one of the sicknesses of Roman culture."[89] One symbol of which was the gladiator, that figure of ultimate despair, with its thrill of what became inescapable. A fitting face of civilization.

(ENDNOTES)

1   Karl Kautsky, *Foundations of Christianity*, translated by Henry F. Mins (New York: S.A. Russell, 1953), p. 109.

2   Noel Lenski, *Failure of Empire: Valens and the Roman State in the Fourth Century A.D.* (Berkeley: University of California Press, 2002), p. 369.

3   Aldo Schiavone, *The End of the Past: Ancient Rome and the Modern World*, translated by Margery J. Schneider (Cambridge: Harvard University Press, 2000), e.g. p. 175.

4   Edward Gibbon, *The History of the Decline and Fall of the Roman Empire* (London: Thomas Figg, 1827), Vol. VI, p. 223.

5   Quoted by Herbert J. Muller, *Freedom in the Ancient World* (New York: Harper & Brothers, 1961), p. 283.

6   Schiavone, *op.cit.*, p. 29.

7   Gibbon, *op.cit.* (Modern Library edition, 1995), Vol. I, p. 437.

8   Lionel Casson, *Everyday Life in Ancient Rome* (Baltimore: The Johns Hopkins University Press, 1998), p. 39.

9   F.W. Walbank, *The Awful Revolution: The Decline of the Roman Empire in the West* (Toronto: University of Toronto Press, 1969), p. 1.

10 Peter Brown, *The Making of Late Antiquity* (Cambridge: Harvard University Press, 1978), p. 31.

11 Peter Sarris, *Empires of Faith: The Fall of Rome to the Rise of Islam, 500–700* (New York: Oxford University Press, 2011), p. 6.

12 Jeremy K. Knight, *The End of Antiquity* (Stroud, Gloucestershire, UK: Tempus, 2007), p. 9.

13 Joseph A. Tainter, *The Collapse of Complex Societies* (New York: Cambridge University Press, 1988), p. 144.

14 *Ibid.*, p. 137.

15 Michael Rostovtzeff, *The Social and Economic History of the Roman Empire* (Oxford: Clarendon Press, 1967), p. 525.

16 Tainter, *op.cit.*, p. 150.

17 Ramsay MacMullen, *Changes in the Roman Empire* (Princeton, NJ: Princeton University Press, 1990), p. 68.

18 Solomon Katz, *The Decline of Rome and the Rise of Medieval Europe* (Ithaca, NY: Cornell University Press, 1955), p. 31.

19 Sarris, *op.cit*, p. 75.

20 Stewart Perowne, *The End of the Roman World* (New York: Thomas Y. Crowell Company, 1967), p. 14.

21 Gilbert Murray, *Five Stages of Greek Religion* (London: Watts & Co., 1935), Chapter IV, "The Failure of Nerve."

22 Carlin A. Barton, *The Sorrows of the Ancient Romans: The Gladiator and the Monster* (Princeton, NJ: Princeton University Press, 1995), p. 98.

23 MacMullen, *op.cit.*, p. 117.

24 Katz, *op.cit.*, p. 41.

25 MacMullen, *op.cit.*, pp. 148–150.

26 Brown, *The Making of Late Antiquity*, *op.cit.*, p. 40.

27 Michael Grant, *The Fall of the Roman Empire* (London: Weidenfeld and Nicolson, 1990), p. 176.

28 Peter Brown, *Power and Persuasion in Late Antiquity: Towards a Christian Empire* (Madison: The University of Wisconsin Press, 1992), p. 52.

29 Galen, *On the Passions and Errors of the Soul*, translated by Paul W. Harkins (Columbus: Ohio State University Press, 1963), p. 66.

30 Kenneth Clark, *Civilisation: A Personal View* (New York: Harper & Row, 1969), p. 31.

31 E.T. Salmon, *The Nemesis of Empire* (New York: Oxford University Press, 1974), p. 61.

32 David Lambert, "The Barbarians in Salvian's De Gubernatione Dei," in Stephen Mitchell and Geoffrey Greatrex, eds., *Ethnicity and Culture in Late Antiquity* (London: Duckworth, 2000), p. 104.

33 Walter Goffart seems to lead the way here. See his *Barbarians and Romans, A.D. 414–584: The Techniques of Accommodation* (Princeton, NJ: Princeton University Press, 1980).

34 Salmon, *op.cit.*, p. 48.

35 David S. Potter, *The Roman Empire at Bay A.D. 180–395* (New York: Routledge, 2004), p. 528.

36 Ralph W. Mathisen, "Violent Behavior and the Constitution of Barbarian Identity in Late Antiquity," in H.A. Drake, ed., *Violence in Late Antiquity* (Burlington, VT: Ashgate, 2006), p. 32.

37 Tacitus, *The Works of Tacitus*, Vol.II, "A Treatise on the Situation, Manners, and Inhabitants of Germany" (London: George Bell and Sons, 1909), e.g. pp. 300, 308, 312, 342.

38 Rostovtzeff, *op.cit.*, p. 498.

39 J.B. Bury, *A History of the Later Roman Empire*, Vol. II (New York: MacMillan and Co., 1889), p. 14.

40 *Ibid.*, Vol. I, p. 97.

41 Peter Brown, *The World of Late Antiquity* (London: Thames and Hudson, 1971), p. 123.

42 Peter Heather, "The Barbarian in Late Antiquity," in Richard Miles, ed., *Constructing Identities in Late Antiquity* (New York: Routledge, 1999), p. 248.

43 *Ibid.*, p. 253.

44 A.H. Merrills, *History and Geography in Late Antiquity* (New York: Cambridge University Press, 2005), p. 56.

45 E.A. Thompson, "Slavery in Early Germany," in M.I. Finley, ed., *Slavery in Classical Antiquity* (Cambridge, UK: W. Heffer & Sons Ltd., 1960), pp 28–29.

46 Sarris, *op.cit.*, p. 34.

47 Quoted in Kautsky, *op.cit.*, p. 58.

48 Tainter, *op.cit.*, p. 147.

49 Emanuele Papi, "A New Golden Age?" in Simon Swain and Mark Edwards, eds., *Approaching Late Antiquity* (New York: Oxford University Press, 2006), p. 3.

50 Kautsky, *op.cit.*, p. 144.

51 Tainter, *op.cit.*, p. 58.

52 Salmon, *op.cit.*, p. 81.

53 Rostovtzeff, *op.cit.*, p. 532.

54 A.D. Lee, *From Rome to Byzantium AD 363–565* (Edinburgh: Edinburgh University Press, 2013), p. 214.

55 Robert Knapp, *Invisible Romans* (Cambridge: Harvard University Press, 2011), p. 40.

56 MacMullen, *op.cit.*, p. 267 and MacMullen, *Enemies of the Roman Order: Treason, Unrest, and Alienation in the Empire* (Cambridge: Harvard University Press, 1966), pp. 180–184. Also Brown, *Power and Persuasion in Late Antiquity, op.cit.*, p. 87.

57 Nicholas Purcell, "The Populace of Rome in Late Antiquity," in W.V. Harris, ed., *The Transformations of Urbs Roma in Late Antiquity* (Portsmouth, RI: Journal of Roman Archaeology, 1999), p. 156.

58 Brown, *Power and Persuasion in Late Antiquity, op.cit.*, p. 81.

59 Katz, *op.cit.*, p. 34.

60 Knapp, *op.cit.*, p. 314.

61 Victor Ehrenberg, *Man, State, and Deity: Essays in Ancient History* (New York: Routledge, 2011), p. 15.

62 E.R. Dodds, *Pagan and Christian in an Age of Anxiety* (Cambridge: Cambridge University Press, 1965), p. 80.

63 Glen W. Bowersock, *Selected Papers on Late Antiquity* (Bari: Edipuglia, 2000), pp. 118-119.

64 Ramsay MacMullen, *Christianity and Paganism in the Fourth to Eighth Centuries* (New Haven: Yale University Press, 1997), p. 33.

65 Brown, *The Making of Late Antiquity, op.cit.*, p. 50.

66 Neil Christie, *From Constantine to Charlemagne* (Burlington, VT: Ashgate, 2006), p. 26.

67 Brown, *The World of Late Antiquity, op.cit.*, p. 50.

68 Jack T. Sanders, *Charisma, Converts, Competitors* (London: SCM Press, 2000), p. 8.

69 *Ibid.*, pp. 154-155.

70 Shirley Jackson Case, *The Social Triumph of the Ancient Church* (New York: Harper & Brothers, 1933), p.78. Also L.W. Countryman, *The Rich Christian Church of the Early Empire: Contradictions and Accommodations* (New York and Toronto: The Edwin Mellen Press, 1980).

71 Rostovtzeff, *op.cit.*, p. 509.

72 Bowersock, *op,cit.,* p. 58.

73 Brown, *Power and Persuasion in Late Antiquity, op.cit.*, p. 108.

74 *Ibid.*, p. 103.

75 MacMullen, *Changes in the Roman Empire, op.cit.*, p. 265.

76 Franz Borkenau, *End and Beginning* (New York: Columbia University Press, 1981), p. 21.

77 A.H.M. Jones, *The Decline of the Ancient World* (London: Pearson, 1975), p. 327.

78 Michael Grant, *The Climax of Rome* (New York: Plume, 1970), p. 222.

79 David Rohrbacker, *The Historians of Late Antiquity* (New York: Routledge, 2002), pp. 198-199.

80 Grant, *The Fall of the Roman Empire, op.cit.*, p. 154.

81 *Ibid.*, p. 151.

82 Grant, *The Climax of Rome*, op.cit., p. 242.

83 Bruce Trigger, *Understanding Early Civilizations* (New York: Cambridge University Press, 2003), p. 157.

84 Walter Scheidel, "Human Mobility in Roman Italy, II: The Slave Population," in *Journal of Roman Studies* XCV (2005), p. 64.

85 Sarris, *op.cit.*, p. 31.

86 Niall McKeown, *The Invention of Ancient Slavery?* (London: Duckworth, 2007), p. 59.

87 Knapp, *op.cit.*, p. 157.

88 McKeown, *op.cit.*, p. 59.

89 Barton, *op.cit.*, p. 181.

Industrialism
and Its Discontents:
The Luddites
and Their Inheritors

Nearly two hundred years ago, Mary Wollstonecraft Shelley gave us a classic warning about the hubris of technology's combat against nature. Her late Gothic novel, *Franken-stein, or the Modern Prometheus* (1818), depicts the revenge nature takes upon the presumption of engineering life from the dead. Victor Frankenstein and his creation perish, of course; his "Adam" is as doomed as he is. If this monster cannot be saved by his father/creator, however, today's cyborg/robot/Artificial Intelligence products *do* expect to be saved. For those at the forefront of technological innovation today, there will be no return to a previous, monster-free state.

From our hyper-tech world we can look back to Mary Shelley's time and see the prototype, the arrival of modern techno-industrial reality. Between 1800 and 1820, England underwent the strains, storms, and challenges of the ascendant Industrial Revolution. We are living with the outcome of that decisive battleground time.

Ugo Perone put it this way: "One day the big O with which the Ottocento [the eighteenth century] begins exploded, and philosophy as the great tale of totality started to be abandoned. The age of specializations began...."[1]

Of course, few changes happen overnight. Industrial output had been 'tending' sharply upward since the early 1780s.[2] And one could easily look much further back, to deforestation in Neolithic and Bronze Age times, to find out why many moors and heathlands are now barren.[3] But it was in the early nineteenth century that power was passing from the hands of the titled landowners to those who owned the factories and foundries. Much more fundamentally, the time and space of social existence were fundamentally altered. As the equality of all citizens before the law began to emerge, so did the reality of an unprecedented subjugation or domestication.

Nothing in the canon of the (fairly recent) Enlightenment, with its claims and promises, had prepared anyone for this. The road to complete mastery of the physical and social environments was indeed opening, as the industrial system became, in Toynbee's words, "the sole dominant institution in contemporary Western life."[4] The picture thus presented was laden with far more pain and absence than promise.

With the nineteenth century begins the winter of the West.[5] Spengler's conclusion is more apt than he knew. It was not a beginning, but the beginning of the end. Dickens' depiction of Coketown in *Hard Times* did much to capture the repercussions of industrialism: the new mass society, ruled by the regime of the factory and its pace, its polluted and despoiled landscape, its inhabitants anonymous and dehumanized. Spengler saw how "the machine works and forces the man to cooperate," rending nature beneath him as this "Faustian" machine passion alters the face of the Earth.[6]

There was a long lead-in to the pivotal developments, a long process of mechanization and privatization. In England, more than six million acres of open field and common pasture were enclosed between 1760 and 1844.[7] The pressures of the new industrial society were increasing enormously, pushing the dispossessed relentlessly toward the despotic mills and mines. New power-driven shearing frames and fully mechanized spinning machines encroached on the relative autonomy of family-based handloom weavers, for example. By the 1820s the pace of change was dizzying.

Especially in the late eighteenth century, Enlightenment theories of rights were advanced as arguments against severe challenges to popular prerogatives. Although the dawn of 1789 had been a moment of great promise, the early idealism of the French Revolution was betrayed by authoritarian terror. In the first years of the nineteenth century, however, "the solidarity of the community [and] the extreme isolation of the authorities" were still political realities.[8]

At issue, in an unprecedented way, is a new state of being, untouched by political claims and reform efforts: a world becoming decisively independent of the individual. The quantum leap in division of labor which is industrialism means the generic interchangeability of parts—and people. From identity and particularity to the stage, in Joseph Gabel's term, of "morbid rationalism."[9] Michel Foucault noted that up to the end of the eighteenth century, "life does not exist: only living beings."[10] The stakes were as high as they could be, the ensuing struggle a world-historical one in this first industrializing nation. It's clear that Emile Durkheim had it entirely wrong when he proclaimed, "that in the industrial societies...social harmony comes essentially from the division of labor."[11]

The march of the factories was a sustained attack on irregular work routines, in favor of the time-disciplined work environment.[12] Centralized production aimed at control over recalcitrant and decentralized workers. By its nature it demanded discipline and regimentation.

Heretofore the customary and numerous holidays from work were supplemented by the celebration of Saint Monday, a day of recovery and play following a typical weekend's drinking. Enshrined in custom and long-standing local tradition, the popular culture—especially among artisans—was independent and contemptuous of authority. Hence factory servitude did not exactly beckon. F.M.L. Thompson noted that it was "extremely difficult to find satisfactory workers," and that "even higher wages were not enough in themselves."[13] For example, the reluctance of weavers (many of them women) to leave their homes has been widely documented.[14]

At least as early as the beginning of the period under review, the beginnings of the destruction of the handicraft artisan and the yeoman farmer could be seen. "The small agricultural cloth-making household units...each so easily identifiable by its tenter of white cloth—would be gone in a few years," observed Robert Reid.[15] Manchester, the world's first industrial city, was one contested ground, among many other English locales, as everything was at stake and the earth was made to shift. By the late 1820s, Thomas Carlyle wrote this summary: "Were we required to characterise this age of ours by a single epithet, we should be tempted to call it, not an Heroical, Devotional, Philosophical, or Moral Age, but above all others, the Mechanical Age."[16]

The widespread "hatred of authority and control"[17] and "general levelling sentiment"[18] meant that resistance was powerful and certainly predated the early nineteenth century. The Northumberland minders destroyed pit-head gear with regularity during clashes with owners, leading to the passage of no fewer than eight statutes directed against such destruction between 1747 and 1816: quite ineffectual statutes, evidently.[19] The briefest sampling reveals the range of late eighteenth-century contestation: the anti-toll Bristol bridge riots of 1793, the great food riot year of 1795 (when groups of women waylaid shipments of corn, and attacked government press gangs seeking to kidnap men for military service), and naval mutinies at Portsmouth and the Nore in 1797, to cite only a few prominent examples.[20]

Machine-breaking and industrial arson soon became focused tactics against the ravages of industrialism, and to some often hard-to-pinpoint degree, against industrialism itself. Such forms of combat are seen among the west England "shearmen and clothing workers, in the Luddite resistance" to the introduction of mechanized devices between 1799 and 1803.[21] This was also the time (1801–1802) of the underground workers' movement known as the Black Lamp, in the West Riding of Yorkshire. Not coincidentally, the 1790s was the golden age of the Lancashire handloom weavers, whose autonomy was the backbone of radical opposition to the factory system.

Marx's idea of revolution was severely limited, confined to the question of which class would rule the world of mass production. But even on those terms he completely failed to predict which groups were most likely to constitute a revolutionary force. Instead of becoming radicalized, factory workers were domesticated to a far greater degree than those who held out against "proletarianization." The quiescence of factory workers is well known. It wasn't until the 1820s that they were first drawn into protest against the progress of the industrial revolution.[22]

"Class" as a social term became part of the language in the 1820s, a by-product of the rise of modern industry, according to Asa Briggs.[23] "It was between 1815 and 1820 that the working class was born," as Harold Perkin had it,[24] but the distinctive consciousness did not, as noted, mean a militant, much less a radical orientation during the pivotal two decades under review. A workerist identity was "scarcely involved" in the Luddite risings between 1800 and 1820.[25]

The most sustained Luddite destruction of newly introduced textile machinery occurred between 1811 and 1816 and took its name from Ned Ludd, a young frame-work knitter in Leicestershire who had an aversion to confinement and drudge work. More than just identification with Ned's famous frame-smashing episode, Luddism may be properly understood as a widely held narrative or vision.[26] At the heart of this shared outlook was a grounded understanding of the corrosive nature of technological progress. The focus is underlined in Robert Reid's wonderfully titled *Land of Lost Content*, wherein he describes a Luddite attack on the hosiery workshop of Edward Hollingsworth on the night of March 11, 1811. Having successfully breached Hollingsworth's fortified works, frame-breaking, à la Ned, ensued. The armed workers proceeded "selectively. Only the wide machines which knitted the broader, cheaper cloth came under the destructive hammer."[27] Such targeting exhibits a combative hostility to standardization and standardized, mass-produced life, hallmarks of industrial progress writ large.[28]

Byron, the most famous poet of the age, was moved to write, "Down with all kings but King Ludd!"[29] More important was the very widespread support for Luddite actions. Across the area, according to E.P. Thompson, "active moral sanction [was] given by the community to all Luddite activities short of actual assassination."[30] Women did not play a key role in the machine-breaking attacks, but were very much a part of the movement. In the April 1812 assault on the Burton power-loom mill in Middleton, women were conspicuously present; five were charged with riot and breaking windows.[31]

Parallel examples of militancy were the East Anglian bread riots of 1815, and the victorious five-month seamen's strike in the same year that paralyzed coal-shipping ports and the east coast coal trade. Frame-breaking had been made a hanging offense in 1812, and repression hit its high point in 1817 with suspension of habeas corpus rights.

But upon the end of the Napoleonic wars in 1815, a long era began that was decisively centered on political reform (e.g. reform of parliamentary representation) and trade unionism. Unions, then as now, exist to broker the relationship between owners and workers. A more or less scattered, independent and often recalcitrant population becomes combined, represented, and disciplined via unionism.[32] This is much less some kind of conspiracy than an accommodation to the great pressures pushing industrial wage-slavery.

As early as Lord Holland's 1812 efforts to channel Luddite energy in a reform direction, there had been interest in somehow moving it away from its real focus. Luddism had to do with something incomparably more basic than politics and unions, but it failed in its frontal assault. A major late-inning target was John Heathcote's lace factory at Longborough in June 1816, and the Folly Hill and Pentrick risings a year later "can be regarded as the last flicker of Luddism in its desperate, violent and political phase."[33] This last adjective refers to a key aspect of the defeat of machine destruction: its diversion into reform channels.

Oppositional energies could still be found, but from this point on they were more often in evidence in more approved contexts. In Bristol, for example, "gangs of disorderly fellows there assembled, throwing stinking fish, dead cats, dogs, rats, and other offensive missiles" during an election campaign.[34] The "Swing" riots throughout southeast England in 1830–1831 harkened back to anti-industrial militancy. Agricultural laborers resented threshing machines that were turning farms into factories; they resorted to destroying them and burning owners' property.[35] Their direct action and communal organization marked them as agricultural Luddites. Another, and pretty much final, outbreak was the Plug riots in the summer of 1842, when a thousand armed workers held Manchester for several days in a general strike. But the second and third generation came to accept as natural the confinement and deskilling of industrial labor. Only starvation could conquer a few holdouts, notably handloom weavers, terribly outflanked by the factories. What happened, or failed to happen, in the turning-point years of 1800 to 1820 sealed people's fate. The ultimate victor was a new, much deeper level of domestication.

The Luddite challenge to the new order stood out, and continues to inspire. Another, somewhat neglected aspect or current was that of religious utopianism, known as millenarianism. This movement (or movements) shed virtually all association with traditional religious belief. It was distant from that agent of social control, the Church of England, and turned its back(s) on the C of E's main rival, Methodism (a.k.a. Dissenting or Non-Conformist). The millennials were anti-clerical and even at times anti-Christian.[36] They promised a vast transformation; their prophets threatened to "turn the world upside down," similar to the aims of secular revolutionaries.[37] Millenarianism was "directed to the destruction of existing society," and the reigning authorities believed in the possibility that it "might be sufficient to spark off the explosive mixture of social discontent and radical sentiment" then prevailing.[38]

The Methodist leadership recoiled in horror from the Luddite momentum and likewise from the many faces of millenarian extremism, some number of which were breakaways from Methodism. The Primitive Methodist Connexion was steadily growing, along with the "magic Methodists" of Delamere Forest, and the "Kirkgate Screamers" of Leeds, among the many disaffected offshoots.[39] Some of these (and other similar groups) were explicitly referred to as Ranters, recognizing a link to the Ranters (and Diggers) of the seventeenth-century millenarianist rebellion. Already in the 1790s "cheap reprints of long-buried works of Ranter and Antinomian [literally, anti-law] complexion" were circulating.[40]

The Scottish Buchanites, followers of Elspeth Simpson Buchan, wished to hold all things in common and rejected the bonds of official marriage. The Wroeites were largely wool-combers and handloom weavers, fighting against the extinction of their crafts. The more numerous Muggletonians, led by the tailor Ludovic Muggle, offered a refuge to the oppressed and excluded. Among the myriad groups and sects a range of millennial faiths can be found. Joanna Southcott, with her thousands of Southcottians, was a feminist—but not a radical one. Some of her flock, like Peter Morison and John Ward, were on the fiery side; in 1806 Morison preached the confiscation of "all the property and land belonging to the rich."[41] Richard Brothers of the New Jerusalem proclaimed that "now is the whore of Babylon falling" and the future will see "no more war, no more want."[42] Robert Wedderburn, a black sailor, attracted the "most extreme and impoverished radicals" to his London chapel.[43]

The millenarian impulse was by no means an isolated, cranky, or unrepresentative passion. In the 1790s it emerged "on a scale unknown since the seventeenth century," judged E.P. Thompson.[44] "From the 1790s to at least the 1830s radical millenarianism could pose a real threat" to the dominant system, precisely because it did not accept the ruling paradigm or participate within it.[45] It was an active critique of the deep assumptions of the ruling order.

Domestic servants and small shopkeepers were among the adherents, as well as artisans and other dispossessed craftspeople who were the spearhead of the Luddite ranks. And in 1813 a New Connexion minister, George Beaumont, was charged with inspiring the Luddite attacks in the Huddersfield area.

Thomas Spence was an influential, apocalyptic figure who found inspiration in the seventeenth-century visionaries. He reprinted a Digger tract from that era by Gerald Winstanley, and likewise attacked private property as standing against God's common storehouse. Spence was convinced that "God was a very notorious Leveller" and that it was possible and necessary for humble men to turn the world upside down.[46]

Alas, the world wasn't turned upside down. The civilizing machine persevered through the storms. Religion, in its usual role, taught respect for authority and had a new weapon in its arsenal: the evangelical revival's campaign for industrial discipline.

William Blake, of "dark Satanic mills" fame, was an enigmatic, idiosyncratic figure who certainly played a part in this period. Not fully a millenarian or a Romantic either, Blake took as his central theme "the need to release the human spirit from bondage."[47] Starting from an orientation toward class struggle, Blake ultimately opposed kingship, and rulership itself.[48]

His *Songs of Experience* (1790s) point in a radical and millenarian direction, and he provided a radical critique of the limits of Swedenborgianism. But Blake can be characterized more as a Jacobin reformer than a revolutionary millennial. Consistency may be hard to find overall, though some observations, rendered in his own inimitable style, hit the mark. He found the factory and the workhouse terribly wrong and, as with the Luddites, saw the destruction of traditional workmanship as the end of working people's integrity. Mechanized time was a particularly important target: "the hours of folly are measured by the clock, but of wisdom: no clock can measure," for example.[49]

Blake's outlook on both nature and women has to be seen as quite flawed. His antifeminism is hard to miss, and there is a contempt for nature, as female and therefore secondary to the male. Social harmony is a major goal, but harmony or balance with nature, as championed by the Romantics or William Morris, for instance, was of no interest to Blake.[50] He desired the "Immediate by Perception or Sense at once,"[51] but it did not occur to him to ground this desire in the non-symbolic natural world.

E.P. Thompson clearly went too far in asserting, "Never, on any page of Blake, is there the least complicity with the kingdom of the Beast."[52] More accurate was his appraisal that few "delivered such shrewd and accurate blows against the ideological defenses of their society."[53]

The first two decades of the nineteenth century were the heart of the Romantic period, and the course of this literary movement reflects what took place socially and politically in those years. At the beginning,

Coleridge, Wordsworth, Shelley, and others gave voice to "an explosion of millenarial and apocalyptic enthusiasm for the new dawn."[54] Writing in 1804, Wordsworth recalled the exhilaration of ten years or so earlier, when the French revolution announced a new world and the factory system had not yet metastasized: "Bliss was it in that dawn to be alive, /But to be young was very Heaven!"[55] In its first bloom especially, Romanticism sought to reconcile humans and nature, consciousness and unconsciousness. As Northrup Frye put it, "the contrast between the mechanical and the organic is deeply rooted in Romantic thinking."[56] René Wellek noted that such thinking could be seen as "an upsurge of the unconscious and the primitive."[57]

Events, soon to be defined by Marx and other industrializers as Progress, undid optimism and a sense of possibilities, as we have seen. Sunny Enlightenment predictions about the perfectibility of society were already turning to ashes, as people became increasingly separated from nature and entered the state of modern, industrial slavery. A great sense of disappointment overtook the earlier aspirations, which were rapidly being destroyed by each new advance of industrial capitalism. From this point onward, disillusionment, ennui, and boredom became central to life in the West.

William Wordsworth acknowledged the existence and importance of a spirit of wild nature, which Blake resisted in him. Wordsworth was particularly moved by the decline of the domestic or pre-industrial mode of production and its negative impact on the poor and on families.[58] Privation, a sense of what has been lost, is a key theme in Wordsworth. His well-known decline as a poet after 1807 seems linked to the pessimism, even despair, that began to get the upper hand. He saw that the Enlightenment enshrining of Reason had failed, and he abandoned Nature as a source of value or hope.

Samuel Taylor Coleridge's anguish at the erosion of community brought surrender and drug addiction. His *Rime of the Ancient Mariner* testifies to the erosion of values in the absence of community. His "Michael" poems completed a series on abandonment and meaningless loss. A major poet who collapsed back into Anglican orthodoxy—as did Wordsworth—and nationalist conservatism.

One who kept the liberatory Romantic flame burning longer was Percy Bysshe Shelley. Influenced by the anarchist William Godwin,

Shelley's *Queen Mab* (1813) contains these lines:

> Power, like a desolating pestilence,
> Pollutes whate'er it touches; and obedience,
> Bane of all genius, virtue, freedom, truth,
> Makes slaves of men, and, of the human frame,
> A mechanized automaton. (III, 176)[59]

Shelley's *Mask of Anarchy* (1819) is an angry call to arms following the government assault on protestors, known as the Peterloo Massacre (e.g. "Rise like Lions after slumber/In unvanquishable number").[60] But he too flamed out, lost his way. The *Hyperion* project was dropped, and a major work, *Prometheus Unbound*, presents a confusing picture. By 1820 his passion had been quelled.

Of aristocratic lineage, George Gordon, Lord Byron was a lifelong radical. He spoke out against making frame-breaking a capital offense, and defended the impoverished. His brazen, bisexual behavior shocked a society he despised. With *Childe Harold* and *Don Juan*, transgressors escaped their "just desserts" and instead were glamorized. Byron saw nature as a value in itself; his nature poetry is correspondingly instinctive and immediate (as is that of his contemporary, John Keats).

He was the most famous of living Englishmen but said goodbye to England in 1816, first to join forces with Carbonari partisans in Italy, and later on the side of Greek rebels, among whom he died in 1824. "I have simplified my politics into an utter detestation of all existing governments," he had declared.[61]

Dino Falluga recognized that some celebrated the death of Byron and what he represented. Victorian novelist Edward Bulwer-Lytton wrote a few decades after the fact that thanks to Byron's death the culture was finally able to grow up. It "becomes accustomed to the Mill," rather than quixotically defending the Luddites as Byron did.[62] Expectations of change did indeed die with Byron, if not before. There was frustration with individual disappointments, also with a generalized, now chronic condition. Now the solitary poet becomes a true fixture, true to the reality that the poet—and not only the poet—is losing the last resource, one's own authority over oneself. Another deep loss of this era, perhaps the deepest. The age of no more autonomy, of no more hope of making things basically different.

The Gothic novel represents the dark side of Romanticism. It had been launched decades earlier, with Horace Walpole's anti-Enlightenment *The Castle of Otranto* (1764), and outlived Romanticism considerably. Its rise suggests resistance to the ideas of progress and development. The more psychoanalytically inclined see the Gothic as a return of what had been repressed: "a rebellion against a constraining neoclassical aesthetic ideal of order and unity, in order to recover a suppressed primitive and barbaric imaginative freedom."[63]

A common feature of many Gothic novels is a look backward to a simpler and more harmonious world—a connection to Rousseauian primitivism. Gothic's revolt against the new mechanistic model for society often idealizes the medieval world (hence the term Gothic) as one of organic wholeness. But this rather golden past could hardly be recognized through the distorting terror of the intervening years. Gothic ruins and haunted houses in print reflected the production of real ruins, real nightmares. The trauma of fully Enlightened modernity finds its echo in inhuman literary settings where the self is hopelessly lost and ultimately destroyed. The depravity of Matthew Lewis' *The Monk*, hailed by the Marquis de Sade, comes to mind, as does Mary Shelley's *Frankenstein*, which demonizes its own creation. Soon, however, the Gothic became as mechanistic a genre as the social order it rejected. Its formulaic products are still being churned out.

The formation of malleable character, adaptable to the regimen of industrial life, was of obvious importance to the various managers in the early nineteenth century. Hence a key argument for support of schools was that they were "a form of social insurance."[64] In Eric Evans' summary, "By 1815 the argument was not whether education for the lower orders was proper but how much should be provided."[65]

The dinnerware manufacturer Thomas Wedgwood wanted a rigorous, disciplinary system of education and tried to enlist Wordsworth as its superintendent. His response, in *The Prelude*, includes these stinging lines:

> The Guides, the Wardens of our faculties,
> And Stewards of our labor, watchful men
> And skillful in the usury of time,
> Sages, who in their prescience would controul
> All accidents and to the very road
> Which they have fashion'd would confine us down,
> Like engines...[66]

Private, usually Christian, schools received some government funding, but a national system of education was rather slow in arriving.

Food rioters, anti-enclosure fence-breakers, not to mention Luddites, could end up on the gallows, but a modern uniformed police force was not implemented much earlier than was a standardized school system. While those in authority had great need of law enforcement, they faced the deep-rooted hostility of the majority. Prevailing sentiment held that personal morality should not be subject to scrutiny by the armed force of society and law. Police were opposed as "paid agents of the state who informed on their neighbors and interfered in private life."[67]

Uniformed police were on the streets of London with passage of the Metropolitan Police Act of 1829, but strong antipathy to the new institution persisted. At a political reform rally in Coldbath Fields, London in 1833 a struggle broke out and three officers were stabbed, one fatally. The subsequent coroner's jury brought in a verdict of justifiable homicide.

The change toward formal policing was just one aspect of an enforced social shift already underway. Increased control of mores introduced laws against "public indecency," and other punitive measures were enshrined in the Vagrant Act of 1822. This was part of the transition from "a largely communal to a primarily state-oriented, bureaucratically organized and professionally supported civic culture," in the words of M.J.D. Roberts.[68] Idleness was a mark against the overall industrial future, so the treadmill was introduced. (Idleness among the rich was quite different, needless to say.) Unauthorized fairs were subject to suppression, though they showed considerable staying power; the Vagrant Act of 1824 was aimed at a variety of popular entertainments. The outlawing of "blood sports" like cock-fighting and bull-baiting may be seen as a positive move; but there was no talk of banning hunting of fox, rabbit, and deer by the upper crust.

Driven by the enclosure movement at base, privatization struck on all levels. Domesticity tended to crowd out the social, and happiness became "a fireside thing."[69] Enclosure meant an absolutization of private property; enjoyment was increasingly private and confined. The home itself becomes more specifically divided, isolating family members within the household.[70] Movement is toward segregation of the sexes and identification of women with domesticity. The family and its division of labor become integrated with the trajectory of industry.

Consumer demand for cheap manufactured goods was an under-lying, emergent key to the Industrial Revolution. This "demand" was not exactly spontaneous; new wants were now very widely advertised and promoted, filling the vacuum of what had been taken away. The decline in traditional self-sufficiency was everywhere apparent; beer and bread were now more often bought than brewed and baked at home, for example. Standardized goods—and a standardized national language—were in full flow.[71]

A stronger emphasis on the need for regular, predictable labor is shown by the prevalence of factory clocks, schedules, and timetables; also domestic clocks and personal watches, once luxury items and now consumer necessities. By the 1820s, nostalgic images were being reproduced using the kinds of technology that erased the lost, commemorated world.[72] As a relatively self-sustaining arrangement of life, rural society was ending, fast becoming a commercial item to be wistfully contemplated.

Bulwer-Lytton wrote in 1833 of the ascendant standards of decorum and conformity: "The English of the present day are not the English of twenty years ago."[73] Diversions that many had enjoyed throughout their lives—public drinking, many holidays from work, boisterous street fairs, etc.—were seen as disgraceful and disgusting under the new order.

As the average person was being subdued and tamed, a few were lionized. Industrial modernity ushered in what is so prominent today, celebrity culture. The flamboyant actor Thomas Kean was an early star, but none surpassed the fame of Byron. He was one of the first ever to receive what we would call fan mail, that is, unsolicited letters on a mass scale.[74] Massified life also initiated widespread psychic immiseration. The best seller of 1806 was *The Miseries of Human Life*, testifying to the large-scale anxiety and depression that had already set in, inevitable fruit of modern subjugation.

The door that was forced open decisively between 1800 and 1820, roughly speaking (and I do mean roughly), inaugurated both global warming and an ever-mounting rise in global population. Globalizing industrialization is the motive force behind both developments. A deep-ening technological dimension becomes more and more immersive and defining, driving the loss of meaning, passion, and connection. This trajectory continually reaches new levels, at an ever accelerating rate. As early as the 1950s, new technology was hailed by many as a "Second

Industrial Revolution."[75] In 1960 Clark Kerr and others announced that "the world is entering a new age—the age of total industrialization."[76]

As the nineteenth century waned, William Morris, who disliked all machinery, concluded that "Apart from the desire to produce beautiful things, the leading passion of my life has been and is hatred of modern civilization."[77] His *News from Nowhere* expresses a wonderful reversal of perspective, in which Ellen speaks from a time that has set aside the techno-desolation: "And even now, when all is won and has been for a long time, my heart is sickened with thinking of all the waste of life that has gone on for so many years." "So many centuries, she said, so many ages."[78]

(ENDNOTES)

1   Ugo Perone, *The Possible Present* (Albany: State University of New York Press, 2011), p. 60.

2   T.S. Ashton, *An Economic History of England: The 18th Century*, vol. 3 (London: Methuen, 1955), p. 125.

3   G.W. Dimbleby, *The Development of British Heathlands and their Soils* (Oxford: Clarendon Press, 1962), e.g. pp. 29, 44.

4   Arnold J. Toynbee, *A Study of History*, vol I (London: Oxford University Press, 1934–1958), p. 8.

5   Oswald Spengler, *The Decline of the West*, vol. II (New York: Alfred A. Knopf, 1928), e.g. p. 78.

6   *Ibid.*, p. 503.

7   Harold Perkin, *The Origins of Modern English Society, 1780–1880* (London: Routledge & Kegan Paul, 1969), p. 125.

8   E.P. Thompson, *The Making of the English Working Class* (New York: Vintage Books, 1966), p. 583.

9   Joseph Gabel, *False Consciousness: An Essay on Reification* (Oxford: Basil Blackwell, 1975).

10 Michel Foucault, *The Order of Things* (New York: Vintage Books, 1970), p. 161.

11 Robert N. Bellah, ed., *Emile Durkheim on Morality and Society* (Chicago: University of Chicago Press, 1973), p. 86.

12 Somewhat recent scholarship has challenged Ashton, Landes and others as having over-generalized the irregularity of pre-industrial work habits; e.g. Mark Harrison, *Crowds and History* (New York: Cambridge University Press, 1988), ch. 5, esp. p. 111. But the overall description seems valid.

13 F.M.L. Thompson, *The Cambridge Social History of Britain 1750–1950*, vol. 2 (New York: Cambridge University Press, 1990), pp 129, 130.

14 Ashton, *op.cit.*, p. 117.

15 Robert Reid, *Land of Lost Content: The Luddite Revolt, 1812* (London: Heinemann, 1986), pp. 294-295.

16 Quoted in Ben Wilson, *Decency and Disorder: The Age of Cant 1789–1837* (London: Faber and Faber, 2007), p. 356.

17 *Ibid.*, p. 74.

18 E.P. Thompson, "The Crime of Anonymity," in Douglas Hay et al., eds., *Albion's Fatal Tree: Crime and Society in Eighteenth-Century England* (New York: Verso, 2011), p. 277.

19 Ian R. Christie, *Stress and Stability in Late Eighteenth-Century Britain* (Oxford: Clarendon Press, 1984), pp. 150–151.

20   Nicholas Rogers, *Crowds, Culture, and Politics in Georgian Britain* (Oxford: Clarendon Press, 1998), p. 229.

21   Thompson in Hay et al., *op.cit.*, p. 275.

22   Neil J. Smelser, "Sociological History," in M.W. Flinn and T.C. Smout, eds., *Essays in Social History* (Oxford: Clarendon Press, 1874), pp. 31–32.

23   Asa Briggs, "The Language of 'Class' in Early Nineteenth-Century England," in Flinn and Smout, *op.cit.*, p. 154.

24   Perkin, *op.cit.*, p. 213.

25   Smelser, *op.cit.*, p. 31.

26   Katrina Navickas, "The Search for 'General Ludd': The Mythology of Luddism," *Social History* 30:3 (August 2005).

27   Reid, *op.cit.*, pp. 59–60.

28   The radical impulse in Ireland was diverted into Ribbonism, somewhat like Luddism, but lost in a nationalist emphasis. Simon Edwards "Nation and State," in Zachary Leader and Ian Haywood, eds., *Romantic Period Writings 1798–1832: An Anthology* (New York: Routledge, 1998), p. 125.

29   Kirkpatrick Sale, *Rebels Against the Future: The Luddites and their War on the Industrial Revolution* (Cambridge, MA: Perseus, 1996), p. 17.

30   E.P. Thompson, *The Making of the English Working Class*, p. 585.

31   Rogers, *op.cit.*, p. 238.

32   For the conservative role of unions see John Zerzan, "Who Killed Ned Ludd?" in John Zerzan, *Elements of Refusal* (Columbia, MO: C.A.L. Press, 1999), pp. 205–211.

33   Edward Royle, *Revolutionary Brittania?: Reflections on the Threat of Revolution in Britain, 1789–1848* (Manchester: Manchester University Press, 2000), p. 51.

34   M. Harrison, *op.cit.*, p. 179.

35   Roland Quinault, "The Industrial Revolution and Parliamentary Reform," in Patrick K. O'Brien and Roland Quinault, eds., *The Industrial Revolution and British Society* (New York: Cambridge University Press, 1993), p. 197.

36   J.F.C. Harrison, *The Second Coming: Popular Millenarianism 1780–1850* (New Brunswick, NJ: Rutgers University Press, 1979), p. 10.

37   Iain McCalman, *Radical Underworld* (New York: Cambridge University Press, 1988), p. 61.

38   J.F.C. Harrison, *op.cit.*, pp 50, 77.

39   Eric J. Evans, *The Forging of the Modern State: Early Industrial Britain, 1783–870* (New York: Longman, 1983), p. 53.

40   Iain McCalman, "New Jerusalem: Prophesy, Dissent and Radical Culture in England, 1786–1830," in Knud Haakonsen, ed., *Enlightenment and Religion: Rational Dissent in Eighteenth Century Britain* (New York: Cambridge University Press, 1996), p. 324.

41   J.F.C. Harrison, *op.cit.*, p. 127.

42   Quoted in E.P. Thompson, *The Making of the English Working Class, op.cit.*, p. 118.

43   I. McCalman, *op.cit.*, p. 139.

44   E.A. Thompson, *Making, op.cit.*, p. 116.

45   E. Royle, *op.cit.*, p. 45.

46   I. McCalman, *op.cit.*, p. 63.

47   Shiv Kumar, "The New Jerusalem of William Blake," in Shiv Kumar, ed., *British Romantic Poets* (New York: New York University Press, 1966), p. 169.

48   Michael Ferber, *The Social Vision of William Blake* (Princeton: Princeton University Press, 1985), pp. 191–192.

49 Quoted in *Ibid.*, p. 135.

50 *Ibid.*, pp 83, 86, 99, 105.

51 Quoted in Heather Glen, *Blake's Songs and Wordsworth's Lyrical Ballads* (New York: Cambridge University Press, 1983), p. 206.

52 E.P. Thompson, *Witness Against the Beast: William Blake and the Moral Law* (New York: Cambridge University Press, 1983), p. 229.

53 *Ibid.*, p. 114.

54 Carl Woodring, *Politics in English Romantic Poetry* (Cambridge, MA: Harvard University Press, 1970), p. 47.

55 Quoted in R.W. Harris, *Romanticism and the Social Order* (London: Blandford Press, 1969), p. 178.

56 Northrup Frye, "The Drunken Boat," in Northrup Frye, ed., *Romanticism Reconsidered* (New York: Columbia University Press, 1963), p. 7.

57 René Wellek, "Romanticism Reconsidered," in Frye, *op.cit.*, p. 117.

58 R.W. Harris, *op.cit.*, p. 193.

59 Quoted in *Ibid.*, p. 288.

60 Quoted in *Ibid.*, p. 299.

61 Quoted in *Ibid.*, p. 361.

62 Dino Franco Felluga, *The Perversity of Poetry: Ideology and the Popular Male Poet of Genius* (Albany: State University of New York Press, 2004), p. 133.

63 Maggie Kilgour, *The Rise of the Gothic Novel* (New York: Routledge, 1995), p. 3.

64 A.P. Wadsworth, "The First Manchester Sunday Schools," in Flinn and Smout, *op.cit.*, p. 101.

65 E. Evans, *op.cit.*, p. 54.

66 E.P. Thompson, "Time, Work-Discipline, and Industrial Capitalism," *Past and Present* 38:1 (1967), p. 97.

67 B. Wilson, *op.cit.*, p. 261.

68 M.J.D. Roberts, "Public and Private in Early Nineteenth-Century London: the Vagrant Act of 1822 and its Enforcement," *Social History* 13:3 (October 1988), p. 294.

69 Robert W. Malcolmson, *Popular Recreations in English Society, 1700–1850* (Cambridge: Cambridge University Press, 1973), p. 156.

70 Jurgen Habermas, *The Structural Transformation of the Public Sphere* (Cambridge, MA: MIT Press, 1989), p. 45.

71 Fiona Stafford, *Local Attachments: The Province of Poetry* (New York: Oxford University Press, 2010), pp. 84–85.

72 David Bindman, "Prints," in I. McCalman, *op.cit.*, p. 209.

73 Quoted in B. Wilson, *op.cit.*, p. 316.

74 Tom Mole, *Romanticism and Celebrity* (New York: Cambridge, University Press, 2009), p. 228.

75 For example, Norbert Weiner, *The Human Use of Human Beings* (London: Eyre and Spottiswoode, 1954).

76 Clark Kerr et al., *Industrialism and Industrial Man* (Cambridge MA: Harvard University Press, 1960), p. 1.

77 Quote in E.P. Thompson, *William Morris: Romantic to Revolutionary* (New York: Pantheon Books, 1977), p. 125.

78 William Morris, *News from Nowhere* (New York: Routledge, 1970), p. 176.

PART II: SITUATIONS

A few observations on the current landscape, the onrushing emptiness here in the technosphere and approaches—false and otherwise—to healing it. Everywhere things are getting starkly worse, a state of all-consuming crisis that needs much better examination than what's on offer. Better than what is generally allowed to be said.

Next What?

Next Nature "refers to the nature produced by humans and their technology." The prevailing attitude of Next Nature is "techno-optimism."

What is the nature of this "Nature" and what are the grounds for the optimism?

I'll start by citing some recent technological phenomena and what they seem to indicate about the nature and direction of our technoculture. We're already increasingly inhabitants of a technosphere, so let's look at some of its actual offerings.

A virtual French-kissing machine was unveiled in 2011. The Japanese device somehow connects tongues via a plastic apparatus. There is also a type of vest with sensors that transmits virtual "hugs." From the Senseg Corporation in Finland comes "E-Sense" technology, which replicates the feeling of texture. Simulating touch itself! Are we not losing our grounding as physical beings as these developments advance?

In some nursing homes now, the elderly are bathed in coffin-shaped washing machines. No human touch required. And as to the mourning process, it is now argued that online grieving is a better mode. Less intrusive, no need to be physically present for the bereaved! There is an iPhone application now available called the "baby cry app." For those who wire their baby's room to be alerted when she stirs, this invention tells parents what the baby's cry means: hungry, wet, etc. (there are five choices). Just think, after about two million years of human parenting, at last we have a machine to tell us why our child is crying. Isn't this all rather horrific?

On a less emotional/interpersonal plane, there are the new cars with GPS built in. "Turn here, turn there." Simple skills like map-reading are eroding, and people are losing their sense of direction and their grasp of the geography of place. Our connection to the Earth (e.g. recognizing landmarks) diminishes further in the dematerializing techno-world. Push a button and the sensor-equipped vehicle parks itself or avoids collisions. We can be inert, skill-less pods, along for the ride.

"Some new technologies like Facebook or mobile phones can actually help people to live a more natural, tribal existence," proclaims Next Nature's website. But how can one not notice that the more society is dominated by technology, the *less* "natural" or "tribal" our existence becomes? In the U.S., according to many studies, people are increasingly atomized and adrift. Levels of isolation are growing at a shocking pace. Since the mid-1980s, for example, the average adult has 50 percent fewer friends and visits friends less often. The number with no friends at all has tripled since the mid-1980s. We are connected to our machines much more than to others (or to the Earth). Facebook "friends"—often individuals one has never even met—is a bitter joke.

Andrew Keen, a CNN writer, authored "How Our Mobile Phones Became Frankenstein's Monster" (February 28, 2012), about personal disempowerment and growing smartphone addiction. In a fragmented, isolated techno-scape, many cling to their phones as to life rafts, but the devices mostly connect nowhere to nowhere. Leaving aside the surveillance capability and brain cancer threat represented by mobile phones, they are more emblematic of an empty life-world than of anything "natural" or "tribal."

«

There is a ton of research showing that Internet immersion is connected to shallow, no-attention-span thinking—the inability to think seriously or in-depth. It has been observed that children now make eye contact much less often, as a function of the number of hours they spend online. Ours is a more and more mediated, disembodied world in which the face-to-face aspect keeps declining, as does direct experience itself.

"A cultural project or phenomenon turns into nature when it becomes potentially or entirely autonomous and uncontrollable" (Next Nature website). If nature means, in effect, technology, then nothing could be further from the truth than this statement. The technological imperative—its inner logic—is the opposite of autonomous and uncontrollable. Technology is born of, and always bears the stamp of domestication. From domestication of animals and plants—and of, ourselves in the process—we entered and began to move ceaselessly along the path of control, within the ethos of domination.

To tame or conquer is the hallmark of technology, as opposed to the realm of tools. Domestication began about 10,000 years ago; various commentators have called it "the worst mistake in human history." Domestication was the shift away from what nature more or less freely gave us, to a colonization of nature. The Earth was put to work, and so many negatives resulted from this fundamental turn: the objectification of women, a life of toil, organized violence, the systematic destruction of nature, and hierarchy, to name a few. Orthodox anthropology now posits that an egalitarian life of sharing was traded, not without huge resistance, for domestication and civilization.

Paul Shepard tells us that nanotechnology, cloning, genetic engineering, etc. were implicit in that first step: the move into domesticated life of ever increasing control and domination. Not exactly autonomous or uncontrollable is the ensuing trail of technological systems. Not exactly free or wild. More control, and always more work.

Technology is never separable from culture, and this relationship is deeply revealing. A society's technology is the physical incarnation of that society. The primary values and choices of a culture or society can be read in its technology.

In very early, non-complex societies we find simple tools, which express values such as equality and autonomy. Tool-based technology is visible, transparent, and accessible; anyone is potentially capable of fashioning, say, stone tools. Early technological processes imply other values such as playfulness, intimacy, and flexibility. In contrast, modern technology expresses, generally speaking, a near total dependence on experts, and standardization, coldness, lack of individuality.

Technology is never a neutral tool. It is rather a socio-cultural dimension, always political in the sense of representing choices—consciously made or not. And choices are not made consciously, by the way, when technology is thought of as neutral and non-political.

"Over time, the expanding influence of humanity on Earth has replaced old nature with next nature." This formulation makes it sound like a seamless, natural process because it leaves out the intervention of a basic social institution. Domestication changed everything, not some abstract "humanity." It is social institutions, and their corresponding technologies, that specifically impact nature.

Take population, for example. There are two pronounced spikes in the human record: the first upon the arrival of domestication globally, and the second about two hundred years ago, with the Industrial Revolution. These jumps in population growth, establishing ever higher levels, correspond to the emergence of two social institutions. Some of us argue that the solution to unnatural population growth is to remove the two primary causal factors, domestication, and industrialism. The call for more technology only adds to the problem since both social institutions are necessary for the existence and growth of technology or "Next Nature." "Evolution goes on"—but in a bad direction.

"We are certainly as opposed to species loss, habitat destruction, and global warming as anyone else." But again, developing the techno-future is based on the systematic destruction of the unbuilt world, on global industrialization. What else enables it? The call for "increased diversity" is completely hollow. Not only are species, languages, and indigenous cultures being sacrificed. the general cultural homogenization is overtaking diversity. Increasingly, the malls, airports, apartments, et al. become identical in a globalizing world. Techno-industrial life grows flatter, textureless, and standardized. Perhaps most important: technology is the same everywhere.

Is it a coincidence that as the techno-culture crowds out everything else, we see growing pathologies in society? In the U.S., tens of millions of people need addictive drugs to sleep, to have sex, to counter anxiety and depression. Meanwhile the shooting sprees—rampage killings in schools, family workplaces, and shopping malls—are daily occurrences. The emptiness and desolation are palpable, bringing continually worsening symptoms.

In today's mass techno-society, community has all but disappeared. And without social bonds and solidarity, anything can and does happen. Virtual "community" is a mockery of actual, face-to-face community, where individuals can be accountable and responsible.

Technology is forever promising solutions. We live in an age where technology fills an ideological vacuum, as political ideologies fade in significance. But by and large, the solutions address problems that were created by technology in the first place—a fact we are not supposed to notice. (Think of diseases spread by intercontinental travel, oil spills, or nuclear power disasters, for instance—and even those diseases that did not exist prior to domestication, including virtually all infectious and degenerative diseases.)

The German sociologist Ulrich Beck argues in his "risk society" thesis that disasters are a built-in feature of complex society. Global warming, the biggest disaster of all, evidently is a function of the growth of global industry. The more factories, the higher the temperature. Again, just what does onrushing technology rest upon? There is an intimate connection between a mobile phone and the destruction, not of illusory "Next Nature," but of billions of years' worth of natural systems that have made life on Earth possible.

Fredric Jameson wrote, somewhat famously, that "Postmodernism is what you get when the modernization process is complete and nature is gone for good." Postmodern culture is indeed, in my opinion, a surrender of this kind: let's just accept the erasure of the natural world and go on from there. In IBM's watchword: "Let's Build a Smarter Planet." We should accept the inevitable success of the cyber/cyborg/digital/ virtual/ information technology juggernaut, not think about what "advanced" society is really advancing toward.

But we know what the fullness of the technological project has brought us. Since Emile Durkheim in the nineteenth century we've known, for example, that modern industrial cities breed much higher rates of suicide and madness. Reams of empirical studies and a century or two of social theory have noticed that modernity produces increasingly shallow and instrumental relationships, amid a life-world that is barren and isolating.

Recently, a friend who is an emergency medical professional told me of calls received during the holiday season, from those who don't have a health emergency. "I think I might be having a heart attack," for example, in order to get a visit—in order to have some human contact.

Do we really want to push all this even further? Life, health, freedom, community need a different direction.

For thousands of generations we lived in band society. Before tribalism, this form of community—perhaps the only actual form that has existed—featured the face-to-face society that consisted of fewer than a hundred people. Mass society of course erased this and so much more.

Novelist Kurt Vonnegut, in a 1973 interview, rejected the claims of modern techno-society, in favor of band society. "Human beings will be happier...when they find ways to inhabit primitive communities. That's my utopia. That's what I want for me." I, too, want to go in that direction. We need a new paradigm, a new vision, which would involve a radical de-centralization, a move away from the ever more integrating world system. Not alter-globalization, a new catch-phrase on the Left, but anti-globalization based on anti-authoritarian perspectives.

More than that we need to start de-domesticating ourselves and re-skilling ourselves. Reconnecting with the Earth in a literal sense. All of us are domesticated but we can start the process of transition. Toward immediacy, wholeness, vitality. It won't be easy but if a growing number becomes involved in such a move the ways and means can be found. I think that a growing number may be feeling the need for such a new direction.

There are no blueprints. We will figure out our paths when our goals can be seen and discussed. As we find each other, the necessary public conversation will begin and the effort to go forward together may ensue. No guarantees, but worth the liberating journey!

Blown Away:
Guns and "Random" Mass Shootings — An Interview With John Zerzan

n recent years, there have been a number of mass shootings throughout North America, a phenomenon which is becoming increasingly normalized in modern society. John Zerzan has written and spoken extensively about this phenomenon of shootings, never shying away from the difficult subjects and questions that many others actively avoid.

Interview by Comrade Black for *Profane Existence*

PE: *I remember you once saying on your radio show that when the media talks about mass shootings they use a set of buzzwords and often present it as though these acts are incomprehensible. Can you explain what you meant and why this is problematic?*

Zerzan: First, let me say that my focus has been on the unprecedented rise in what are commonly called "random" multiple shootings; those that, as you say, are presented as incomprehensible. Of course they are not incomprehensible and speak to the nature of modern mass society. They are deeply symptomatic of the growing isolation, a product of the disappearance of community. Society becomes rapidly more technological and—contrary to the propaganda claims of the tech agenda —people are ever more adrift and lonely. With less and less to hang on to unspeakable things happen.

PE: *Often mass shootings get blamed on mental health, yet many of these killers had no history of known mental illness?*

Zerzan: Yes, most of the shooters have no history of mental illness. More often one reads what has become a kind of cliché description: 'he was the quietest guy, very nice, never missed work or made trouble, etc.'

PE: *A while back there was an article about kids being bored by mass shootings. Do you think they have become part of the spectacle? Or are they the cracks?*

Zerzan: It's possible that as these multiple homicide acts become almost daily occurrences events they are tuned out or even become boring. Think what else is routinely tuned out among the common horrors of civilization...

PE: *I saw a feminist blogger recently write that all these shootings have one thing in common, that the perpetrators are all men. What's your take?*

Zerzan: Not all the shooters are male. A horrible part of the phenomenon in recent years has been family slaughters, including mothers murdering their children.

PE: *I have heard you say that mass shootings are a phenomenon that appears to be unique to both the modern times and certain parts of the world? What is the connection between privilege and this type of violent act?*

Zerzan: Roughly speaking, these rampage killings happen in the more technological societies and are spreading from the U.S. to other technologically advanced countries. Thus one wonders how 'advanced' or 'privileged' these places really are. In terms of individuals it is less often poorer people committing theses acts, more likely white suburbanites, with some exceptions.

PE: *Ever since Chris Dorner opened fire killing a couple cops, more people are beginning to target the police. As an anarchist, what do you make of this?*

Zerzan: Police brutality and the militarization of the cops seems to be increasing. So, not a big surprise that more folks would strike back.

PE: *Another interesting aspect of the more recent shootings, starting with Dorner, is that the killers used Facebook or other social media to post statements before committing their killings. I am certain this will justify increased profiling and surveillance. What are your thoughts on this?*

Zerzan: Social media usage is of course extremely widespread so we see more use of it by shooters e.g. the Isla Vista killer recently.

PE: *Layla AbdelRahim writes about how politeness and manners are a form of civilized violence that helps to hide the violence of our society. We live in a* *horribly violent culture that pretends the violence doesn't exist; what do you make of these outbursts of very public violence in the spectacle of polite society?*

Zerzan: Layla refers to how domestication represses the violence, if less effectively these days, eh? The violence is less hidden than ever but denial reigns and the 'solutions' put forth are very superficial. For example, gun control laws which miss the basic reality. That is, guns have always been very prevalent in this country, since colonial times in fact. But the shooting rampages as a common phenomenon is quite recent historically. A year before Adam Lanza killed twenty-some children at a school in Connecticut he called Anarchy Radio to tell of a chimpanzee who attacked its owner. The chimp had been dressed in human clothes, fed human food, provided with TV—and snapped because of the degrading domestication it was subject to. The bitter irony was that Lanza himself snapped and killed two dozen people about a year later.

PE: *When Ted Kaczynski was arrested as the Unabomber, you wrote him letters and visited him in jail; how do his acts of violence differ from these others? Is it simply a difference in ideology? What can we learn from "Uncle Ted's" actions?*

Zerzan: Kaczynski's acts were in no way random. They were part of an exclusively anti-technology campaign.

PE: *Is there a connection between how we as a society treat animals and the land with this type of violence?*

Zerzan: I think it's quite reasonable to see the <u>mass cruelty of industrialized agriculture</u>—to use a big example of how animals are treated—as cheapening life in general and thus contributing to these explosions of violence among humans.

PE: *I remember when the Columbine shooting happened which seemed to be one of the first, followed by another high school shooting in Taber, Alberta not far from where I grew up only a week or two later. As a kid in a high school that was tormented and bullied nearly to the point of committing suicide myself, having a couple kids pick up guns and shoot back was something I paid close attention to. But things didn't seem to get better in the aftermath; rather kids like me were treated like we were all potential psychopaths and nothing else really changed.*

Zerzan: Bullying is one triggering factor in some of the mass killings. But bullying is nothing new whereas there is something unprecedented going on as mass society shows such pathologies. I went to a rough high school where, in addition to beatings by some of the priests, there was a fair degree of bullying. No one brought a gun to school and started blowing folks away.

PE: *Fredy Perlman described civilization as a monster that keeps growing and consuming, while telling the story of people who either resisted by running away until the monster caught up to them or by fighting back—often becoming more like the monster they resisted in order to stop it until it collapsed and they took its place as the new monster. How do we resist without becoming recuperated into the machine we seek to destroy?*

Zerzan: Civilization must be attacked at a deep enough level to hit its target. Activism that lacks critique or lacks a qualitatively different vision or paradigm is doomed to be quite limited in my opinion. This means, among other things, that we must not shrink from embracing property destruction, which is hard to co-opt.

PE: *You have argued that technology alienates us further. Are these shootings a symptom of individualism? Capitalism? Lack of nature? Or something else?*

Zerzan: It's all these things even if technology is major—and generally overlooked. Domination is a totality and needs to be seen as such to avoid single-issue reformism.

As Adorno put it, in terms of causes: "It is idle to search for what might have been a cause within a monolithic society. Only that society itself remains the cause."

PE: *You have written about hope, whereas the trend seems to be moving toward nihilism. Where do you find hope in times like these?*

Zerzan: I am hopeful because I see the energy of resistance alive in many places. It has not gone away. And because I think that the system of domination is actually quite hollow and weak. It is plainly losing the allegiance of many on many levels, has no answers to the myriad problems it has created.

‡

Vagaries of the Left

I n February 2012 the progressive columnist Chris Hedges caused quite a stir with "The Cancer in Occupy" (*truthdig*, February 6, 2012), a fairly predictable attack on Black Bloc militancy. It voiced, in general, the perspective of the liberal-moderate-reformist folks who have been mostly predominant in Occupy. Hedges' screed against anarchists and others who "go too far" shows just what anti-authoritarians have been up against and why so few of them, in my experience, have been interested in Occupy. Of course, the Occupy sites are many and varied, it must be added.

Hedges basically counsels that if everyone behaves, then Occupy will continue to succeed, obviously exaggerating the potency of the movement so far. He represents voting, property-respecting, obey-the-rules-of-the-game—unless he's talking about somewhere else. He has lauded rioting and resistance in Greece, for example. His "Cancer" essay is full of gaffes and bloopers, e.g. I am a big voice of Black Bloc, anarchists are full of "a repellent cynicism," etc. It has been critiqued by many, including Peter Gelderloos, magpie, Bobby Whittenberg-James.

I wish to add only a couple of things that have been less developed, or not mentioned by other commentators.

Hedges finds it scandalous that *Green Anarchy* magazine published a brief article years ago (*GA* #5, Spring 2001) criticizing the Zapatista EZLN from the anarchist perspective. As an editor of *GA* at the time, I recall that we weren't thrilled by the piece, but we ran it in the interest of provoking discussion. Chris Hedges is evidently not in favor of open discussion, and neither was the EZLN, which sent us a rather chilling response (*GA* #8, Spring 2002).

If it is scandalous to think critically about what is going on in Chiapas, it is worse, in my opinion, to fail to learn from the evidence, from the record. Over the years I've seen enthusiasm for national liberation-type movements, widely and loudly expressed, fade into silence when such movements became governments or political parties. Do I see this happening in southernmost Mexico? I hope not. Do I support their struggles? Certainly.

But a certain silence has set in, and questions emerge. Remember when Subcomandante Marcos renounced his urban, leftist, intellectual past and embraced indigeneity as the necessary realm of authenticity? Given the recent past of the EZLN, it seems like a long time ago.

In 2005 the Sixth Declaration was proclaimed by the Clandestine Revolutionary Indigenous Committees—General Command of the Zapatista Army of National Liberation. Except for the one word, does any of this hyper-bureaucratic-sounding mouthful seem remotely indigenous? And within this document, there are references to "our Mexico," "our Patria." Is nationalism indigenous? How about such slippery terms or phrases as "The Other Campaign," or "we govern by obeying"? Similarly, "building another way of doing politics, for a program of the Left and for a new constitution"?

For a leftist like Hedges, it is forbidden to wonder about the direction or nature of the EZLN.

But the bulk of "The Cancer of Occupy" consists of quoted opinions of Derrick Jensen, who was once an enemy of civilization. Jensen's opening announcement is that "what they [Black Bloc types] are really doing is destroying the Occupy movement." BB tactics are not only inappropriate; they are "criminal." With his complete intolerance of criticism, Jensen had already cut ties with anarchists. Not "officially," but he's made it pretty clear to many. "I can't stand those people," he wrote in a recent letter to a farmer. It took a few years, but he now seems to be hardly distinguishable from a liberal. The anti-civ bit is a distant memory, used very occasionally, qualified, and tamed. Speaking of tamed, Jensen never seemed to grasp that civilization starts from *domestication*. Can't remember him ever using that word. It is, of course, nothing short of bizarre that *Deep Green Resistance*, a Jensen spin-off, calls for the physical destruction of infrastructure, while DJ recoils in shock and horror from BB militancy. *DGR* has been an attractive idea to some precisely because it is "heavy," portends real action against the machine. When the tactical formations of young people freak out the likes of Jensen, one cannot miss the contradiction: felonious arsons and bombings are called for but Black Bloc is too much (??). DGR projects and at least one of Derrick's recent books are subsidized by the Wallace Fund; that's when things get really bizarre. Major funders of NPR, and named for über-progressive Henry A. Wallace, the Wallace Fund cannot exactly be counted among our anti-civ forces!

Of course, the strategic thinking that Jensen counsels means, I guess, that the DGR will direct the resistance, not undisciplined anarchists. I heard his DGR cohort Lierre Keith speak last year, and in a similar vein, she expressed contempt for ELF and ALF folks, their lack of respect for authority. They would be welcome, however, she said in as many words, as cannon fodder for the DGR authorities, who think like "field generals." I'm not making this up.

In his column, Chris Hedges states: "Black Bloc adherents detest those of us on the organized left." I do detest leftists like Hedges, for obvious reasons. Mainly because they are anti-radical and hence anti-anarchist. That's obvious to me. What should also be obvious is how movements or individuals slide into what should not be acceptable.

A few days after his "Cancer" piece appeared—and a furor ensued—Hedges gave an interview to try to calm the waters (*truthdig*, February 9). Here he admitted that it is anti-civilization and anti-Left ideas, more than Black Bloc, that really set him off. As well they should! That colossal failure known as the Left has, of course, always been a bulwark of civilization. The Left has reason to fear that which means its definitive end.

It should come as no big surprise, given Hedges' progressive orientation, that he opposes anti-civ ideas. Just as it shouldn't be a big jolt to know that Noam Chomsky is similarly exercised by those who question such primary institutions as domestication, civilization, industrialism and mass society—which is fast leading to disaster in every sphere, at every level. And neither should it be big news that Derrick Jensen is more and more a part of the Left and its basic acquiescence in this nightmare we live in.

I was at the beginning of a three-week group speaking tour in India when the Hedges piece broke. Let me add, perhaps as an antidote to Hedges and Jensen, that there are now anarchist groups in India, apparently for the first time. The February visit was my third in the past four years and broke new ground—this time the venues were mostly in the south. To learn more about the tour see www.anhilaal.com, the website for the anti-civ, anti-work, anti-career network in South Asia.

Faster!
The Age of Acceleration

Acceleration is a key fact of human existence today. Time, technology, and modernity are speeding up at an entirely unprecedented rate. These categories or dimensions are becoming parodies of themselves.

Experience, consciousness, our sense of everything is rushed along in a perpetual, hypermediated present—which is not a present. The now has been banished from itself. In the technosphere phase of civilization, our very notion of the present moment has been redefined (mostly) as what flies by on a computer screen. Flying fragments, including us.

Even the perennial Subject-Object question (viz. is there an insuperable alienation between them?) seems to fade in the Age of Acceleration. The subject is ever more insubstantial and disembodied; the object maybe even more so. We are no longer so much surrounded by things as by fleeting virtual images.

Reality seems out of control, in a runaway world. As our daily lives accelerate, less and less happens to us. The power of acceleration, once thought by some to be liberating, is far more widely felt as an enslaving pressure.

Progress "on speed," as it were, heightens the advance of ecological catastrophe. Nature is systematically overburdened, and of course acceleration is its measure.

All of this outraces the ability of thought to come to grips with it. Hartmut Rosa puts it this way: "I fear that we are in danger of running out of claims, hypotheses and theories that are inspiring and challenging for late-modern culture."[1] Though not an acceleration theorist like Rosa, Bruno Latour offers "Why Has Critique Run Out of Steam? From Matters of Fact to Matters of Concern."[2]

But there's no mystery involved. Rosa himself observes that it is "the logic of acceleration that determines the structural and cultural evolution of modern society,"[3] and that "Progress and acceleration were indissolubly linked together from the very beginning."[4] It is clear that growing social and technological complexity, boosted by increasingly interdependent systems and exponentially more powerful computing capacities, constitute the racing reality of mass techno-society.

The reality is more starkly revealed the faster it goes in every sphere. This has not meant, however, that an indictment of the whole is allowed. Such a rejection is perhaps ever more transparently or unavoidably implied, but that perspective is unlikely to be taken seriously. "From the very beginning," in Rosa's words, is an entirely appropriate usage nonetheless. It must be noted in passing that the current nature of this accelerating world is the outcome of the movement of two of the most primary social institutions: division of labor and domestication.

Time has always been a colonizing force. It became a thing, within us, then over us. The emergence and growth of this materiality, time consciousness, corresponds to that of alienation because it is the most primary estrangement. Time is neither neutral nor objective, especially as the depth of the present gives way to the techno-present and our sense of time is re-coded. It leaps forward with all the rest in our epoch, in which even the speed of light, a supposedly unassailable limit, has been surpassed. Time cracks the whip and mocks everything that doesn't keep up. It merges with technological existence and in countless ways proclaims that there is nothing outside either of these dimensions.

Time has literally speeded up. We live in a new global timescape that Ben Agger calls "fast capitalism" and the "total administration of time."[5] Along with time compression goes time famine: it feels like we never have enough time; time is running out. Time is getting more and more scarce. Pressure and stress hound us as we struggle, relying on coffee, energy drinks, and other substances to keep up.[6]

The temporal trajectory has become a permanent but impoverished present. As Baudrillard put it, "Time itself, lived time, no longer has time to take place."[7] Domesticated society has long been temporal in nature, now radically so.[8] The new, post-clock age is very decontextualized, but also shows more of the same progress of time's estrangement from the Earth. The present contracts, but is increasingly all there is. History is evaporating; the past becomes somehow incomprehensible. *Posthistoire: Has History Come to an End?* by Lutz Niethammer poses this well enough. Hervé Fischer concludes, "Cybertime, our time, is tragic. It has no past, no future."[9]

There's no time for depth, engagement, reflective action. The symbolic, which started with time, completes itself as the only presence. Fischer again: "Time has become the very matter of reality."[10] If it is true that oppressive time infiltrates and domesticates at a basic level, the struggle against domination cannot overlook it.

Modern technology is precisely what alters our experience of time. The always-faster colonization of life by technology commands an ever-fluctuating environment in which the self is destabilized and such dichotomies as online-offline, public-private, and work-leisure are made largely irrelevant. The properties of the physical self are reduced, as galloping technology claims to complete and enhance them. Speed is of the essence; computing power means one thing—how fast it is. 2014's Magazine of the Year award went to a tech and business zine called *Fast Company* (*New York Times*, May 1, 2014).

Staring at screens we become "digital interfaces,"[11] approaching a communicative elsewhere which is nowhere. Through the always-developing devices a great indifference to the world is apparent. And why should this be surprising, given how indifferent the world now is to us. A world subdued and rendered uniform, ugly, and lifeless by onrushing technology. Enlightenment modernity, its promises unrealized, is now unrecognizable in key ways. Spengler said that modern times have been "stretched and stretched again to the elastic limit at which [they] will bear no more."[12]

The history of modernity is, on one level, a series of innovations in ever increasing time compression. This mounting technological movement is foundational to the fact that Progress is totalitarian. From urbanization and globalization to the disorienting virtual waves of information, the enclosing pace is relentless.

About a century ago the futurist Marinetti declaimed, "One must persecute, lash, torture all those who sin against speed."[13] Fast-forward to the present: Microsoft Cloud threatens all techno-serfs with the reminder that "The winning edge can boil down to nanoseconds. The Cloud That Helps Win the Race!" (full-page ad, *New York Times*, April 1, 2014). A nanosecond is a billionth of a second. Stock markets around the world now operate on this level. Paul Virilio says that "By accelerating, globalization turns reality inside out like a glove."[14]

Baudrillard stressed that reality comes to an end when real and unreal become indistinguishable. This is the current stage of the catastrophic nature of civilization, which is modernity. And Rosa points to the "acceleration process which is indiscernibly linked to the concept and essence of modernity."[15] Virilio terms this "a culture of desertification,"[16] whose constant uptick guarantees the "liquidation of the world."[17]

All of this operates against mutual and embodied co-presence; this seems to be why (somewhat perversely) all the speeding-up has produced a big increase in sedentariness. Seated before the slight, synthetic glow of the screen as life flies by. As people work faster, because the machines go faster.

"Get.Arts.Fast" is William Grimes' March 21, 2014 *New York Times* offering on abbreviated theater and other performances, shortened to fit the busy schedules of exhausted patrons, as well as their shrinking attention spans. At least accelerating technosphere developments (e.g. Artificial Intelligence, nanotechnology) have so far not managed to keep up with the fantasies of those who actually put their faith in them. Ray Kurzweil's deluded technotopian Singularity dreams get a cinematic comeuppance in the 2014 movie *Transcendence*, by the way.

Somewhere Spinoza wrote that we are immortal here and now, in each instant. And so we continue, in the face of what wants to be overwhelming. Jean-Claude Carriere, asked how he accomplished so many things, responded, "My reply is always the same, and I'm not trying to be funny: 'Because I do them slowly.'"[18] Gifted athletes often remark similarly, on their ability to slow things down.

"All that is solid melts into air," as Marx and Engels characterized the transforming power of industrial capitalism in *The Communist Manifesto*. But what drives the now frantic pulse of transformation was unleashed far earlier. It has indeed gone into overdrive with the Industrial Revolution, but heightening complexity under the sign of domestication is thousands of years older than modern capitalism.

"Don't be evil" is Google's well-known mantra, part of its mission statement. Of course the whole mega-project, of which Google is only the latest tiny part, is the "evil" that is now so virulent. It may appear as the force of destiny, in which case it is time for a new conquest.

(ENDNOTES)

1   Hartmut Rosa, *Alienation and Acceleration* (Natchitoches, LA: NSU Press, 2010), p. 7.

2   Bruno Latour, "Why Has Critique Run Out of Steam? From Matters of Fact to Matters of Concern," *Critical Inquiry*, Winter 2005.

3   Hartmut Rosa, *Social Acceleration*, translated by Jonathan Trejo-Mathys (New York: Columbia University Press, 2013), p. 279.

4   *Ibid.*, p. 321.

5   Ben Agger, "Time Robbers, Time Rebels: Limits to Fast Capital" in Robert Hassan and Ronald E. Purser, eds., *24/7: Time and Temporality in the Network Society* (Stanford, CA: Stanford University Press, 2007).

6   The popular literature is of course extensive. For example: Martin Moore-Ede, *The Twenty-Four-Hour Society: Understanding Human Limits in a World That Never Stops* (Reading, MA: Addison-Wesley, 1993); Thomas Hyland Eriksen, *Tyranny of the Moment* (Sterling, VA: Pluto Press, 2001); Brigid Schulte, *Overwhelmed: Work, Love, and Play When No One Has the Time* (New York: Sarah Crichton Books, 2014).

7   Jean Baudrillard, *The Intelligence of Evil or the Lucidity Pact* (New York: Oxford University Press, 2005), p. 27.

8   For historical analysis see my "Beginning of Time, End of Time" in *Elements of Refusal* (Columbia, MO: C.A.L. Press, 1999) and "Time and its Discontents" in *Running on Emptiness* (Los Angeles: Feral House, 2002).

9   Hervé Fischer, *Digital Shock* (Montreal: McGill-Queen's University Press, 2006), p. 50.

10   *Ibid.*, p. 49.

11   Arthur Kroher, *The Will to Technology and the Culture of Nihilism* (Toronto: University of Toronto Press, 2004), p. 175.

12   Oswald Spengler, *The Decline of the West* I (New York: Alfred A. Knopf, 1926), p. 19.

13   Filippo Tommaso Marinetti, "The New Religion vol. 1—Morality of Speed" in Hartmut Rosa and William E. Scheuerman, eds., *High-Speed Society* (University Park, PA: Pennsylvania State University Press, 2009), p. 58.

14   Paul Virilio, *The Original Accident* (Cambridge: Polity, 2007), p. 51.

15   Rosa, *Alienation and Acceleration, op.cit.*, p. 8.

16   Paul Virilio, *Negative Horizon* (New York: Continuum, 2008), p. 35.

17   *Ibid.*, p. 52.

18   Catherine David, Frederic Lenoir, Jean-Philippe de Tonnac, eds., *Conversations About the End of Time* (New York: Fromm International, 2000), p. 164.

A Word on Civilization
and Collapse

Civilizations have come and gone over the past six thousand years or so. Now there's just one. Various cultures, but a single, global civilization.

Collapse is in the air. We've already seen the failure, if not the collapse, of culture in the West. The Holocaust alone, in the most cultured country (philosophy, music uppermost), revealed culture's impotence.

We have a better idea of what civilization is than we do of what collapse would mean. It's the standard notion: domestication, soon followed by the early, major civilizations of Mesopotamia and Egypt. Domestication, the ground and thrust of civilization per se: the ethos of ever-progressing domination of nature and control in general.

"Nature has not ordained civilization; quite the contrary," as E.J. Applewhite aptly observed. All civilizations have been riven with tensions, and all heretofore have failed. Mayan and Mycenaean civilizations, half a world apart, collapsed simultaneously (if slowly). Egyptian civilization rose and fell four times before it exhausted itself. Arnold Toynbee examined some twenty past civilizations in his massive *A Study of History*. He found that in every case, the cause of collapse was internal, not external.

What may be civilization's deepest tension is brought out in that most radical text, Freud's *Civilization and its Discontents*. For Freud, civilization rests on a primary repression, the source of unconquerable unhappiness: the trading of instinctual freedom and eros for work and symbolic culture. Thus civilization's very foundation, domestication, is the worst of bargains, the basic generator of neurosis. Oswald Spengler underlined the futility of civilization, deciding that it was undesirable, even evil. For Roy Rappaport, maladaptive was the adjective that best described it, though he (like the rest) concluded that smaller, self-sufficient social orders would be as undesirable as they would be impossible to achieve.

In *The Decline of the West*, Spengler noted that the last phases of every civilization are marked by increasing technological complexity. This is strikingly true of planetary culture today, when we also see technology's claims and promises tending to displace those of explicitly political ideology.

William Ophuls' *Immoderate Greatness: Why Civilizations Fail* outlines quite ably the reasons why civilizational failure is inevitable, why the grasping control ethos of domestication comes to its self-defeating end. The book's first sentence also serves very well to announce the fatal illusion that prevails today: "Modern civilization believes it commands the historical process with technological power."

I believe that the fallacy of this belief is becoming clearer to more people. After all, as Jared Diamond put it, "All of our current problems are unintended consequences of our existing technology." In fact, civilization is failing on every level, in every sphere, and its failure equates so largely with the failure of technology. More and more, this is what people understand as collapse.

Complex societies are recent in human history, and certainly this overarching civilization is very different from all that have gone before. The main differences are twofold. Reigning civilization now dominates the entire globe, various cultural differences notwithstanding; and technological invasiveness colonizes to an undreamed-of degree.

Despite this reach and height, the rule of civilization is based on less and less. Inner nature is as ravaged as outer nature. The collapse of human connectedness has opened the door to unimaginable phenomena among lonely human populations. The extinction of species, melting polar ice, vanishing ecosystems, etc. proceed without slowing. Even rather more prosaic aspects of civilization are in decline. Rappaport found that as civilizational systems "become increasingly large and powerful the quality and utility of their products are likely to deteriorate." The massive mid-2014 recall of millions of GM, Toyota, and Ford cars comes to mind. Jared Diamond pointed out that "steep decline may begin only a decade or two after the society reaches its peak numbers."

Enter Peak Oil and its prediction that oil is beginning to run out, signaling the finale of industrial civilization and its ruinous run. The discovery of large reserves of natural gas and new technological processes (e.g. shale gas extraction) may, however, mean that the Peak Oil projection of terminal decline won't begin for many decades. The Oil Drum website, a major Peak Oil forum, went silent in 2008 after an eight-year run, admitting to lack of interest.

There is an understandable, if misplaced, desire that civilization will cooperate with us and deconstruct itself. This mindset seems especially prevalent among those who shy away from resistance, from doing the work of opposing civilization. There is also a tendency to see a dramatic showdown looming, even though history rarely seems to provide us with such a scenario.

Things are dire, and worsening. So we also see more and more pessimism and even surrender, although the former does not always lead to the latter. There will be no big happy ending, counsels the anonymously penned 2011 offering *Desert*. It tells us that the picture of a single global present is an illusion, mirrored by the illusion of a single, global liberated future. But as civilization moves steadily toward a unitary, globalized, highly integrated reality, the first assertion looks demonstrably in error. As for the second, we have no idea what will happen; nonetheless it seems self-evident that either we will overcome the domestication/civilization paradigm or we won't. Not that the struggle will likely be decided in one fell swoop.

Desert presents much in terms of the limits of activism, but is that where all will be decided? The book provides little or no analysis or vision, so ignores what may be crucial: legitimation. I think we are already seeing signs of de-legitimation as awareness grows that civilization is doomed, and civilization's loyalists have no answers to a widening crisis. Things get worse, and civilization makes things worse. It is failing, and we have crucial questions and understanding as to why.

More importantly, a qualitatively different paradigm or vision is possible, and even available. It is not surprising that *Desert* puts forth a lifeboat approach, however unrealistic overall, or that Dark Mountain's Paul Kingsworth, well-known UK environmentalist, flat-out throws in the towel. It looks bad, but civilization's prospects increasingly look even worse: no future. We need to put forth the effort to bring it to an end. The direction is clear: "a return to the normal human condition of lower complexity," in the words of Joseph Tainter (*The Collapse of Complex Societies*). Toward life, health, community, a face-to-face world of robust, re-skilled individuals.

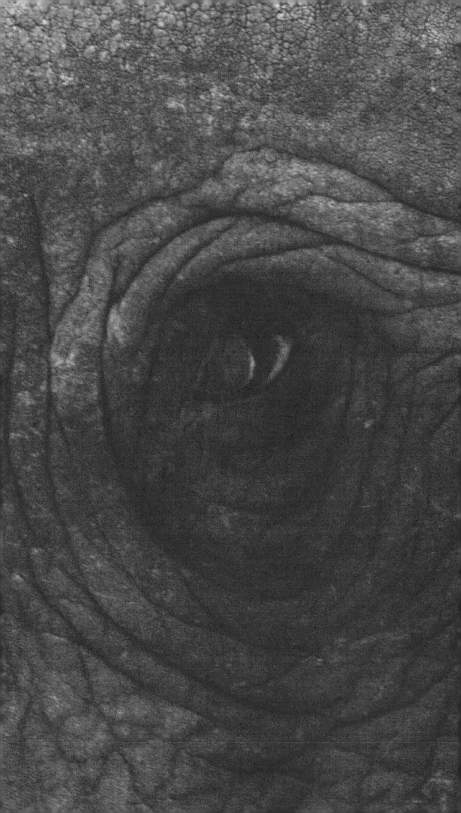

PART III: INSPIRATIONS

There is much to draw on in our struggle to live and to overcome the disease of civilization. The wonderful mystery of non-human animals, consciousness, and the sea, for example. The totality is increasingly, transparently, a death march. Life is so clearly elsewhere and available for new and better ventures!

Animal Dreams

This is the age of disembodiment, when our sense of separateness from the Earth grows and we are meant to forget our animality. But we are animals and we co-evolved, like all animals, in rapport with other bodily forms and aspects of the world. Minds as well as senses arise from embodiment, just as other animals conveyed meaning—until modernity, that is.

We are the top of the food chain, which makes us the only animal nobody needs. Hamlet was very much off the mark in calling humans "the beauty of the world, the paragon of animals." Mark Twain was much closer: "the only animal that blushes. Or needs to."[1] The life form that is arguably least well adapted to reality, that has weaker chances for survival among the at least ten million animal (mostly insect) species. Humans are among the very few mammals who will kill their own kind without the provocation of extreme hunger.[2]

The human species is unique but so is every other species. We differ from the rest no more, it seems, than do other species from each other. Non-human animals have routinely amazing facilities for accomplishing things by acting on information they receive from their environments. They are creatures of instinct, but so are we. As Joseph Wood Krutch asked, "who is the more thoroughly acquainted with the world in which he lives?"[3] Adaptation to one's world is a cognitive process. If we wonder which species is the smartest, the best answer is, most likely: they all are.

I think that Henry Beston is beautifully helpful: "We patronize them for their incompleteness, for their tragic fate of having taken form so far below ourselves. And therein we err, and greatly err. For the animal shall not be measured by man. In a world older and more complete than ours they move finished and complete, gifted with extensions of the senses we have lost or never attained, living by voices we shall never hear."[4]

In the 1980s I knew someone who signed his excellent anti-authoritarian writings and flyers "70 animals." That kind of identification has charmed me ever since. In rather a contrary spirit is the long-prevailing ban on that act of appropriation and greatest sin, anthropomorphism. Correcting this desperate error means that "A monkey cannot be angry: it exhibits aggression. A crane does not feel affection; it displays courtship or parental behavior. A cheetah is not frightened by a lion; it shows flight behavior."[5] Why not take this kind of reductive approach even further and simply remove animals from our vocabulary? This is already underway, if the *Oxford Junior Dictionary* is any indication. The 2009 edition added several techno words like Twitter and mp3, while the names of various animals, trees, etc. had been deleted.[6] Children (and others) have less and less contact with nature, after all.

But there is no substitute for direct contact with the living world, if we are to know what it is to be living. Our own world shrinks and shrivels, cut off from animal culture, from the zones of that shared, learned behavior. What Jacob Uexküll called the Umwelt, the universe known to each species. We need to be open to the community of our beginnings and to the present non-human life-world.

Amphibians have been here for 300 million years, birds for 150 million years. Dragonflies ask no more of the biosphere than they did one hundred million years ago, while *Homo* species, around for not much more than three million years, are the only animals that are—since domestication and civilization—never satisfied, always pursuing new wants.

Might it not be that nature is for the happiness of all species, not just one?[7] We sense something like this as we search for oases of wildness in the vacuum of civilization.

" 'Hope' is the thing with feathers," wrote Emily Dickinson.[8]

We have mainly lost the sense of the presence or aura of animals, of those who inhabit their bodies so wholly, fully. People in traditional indigenous cultures have not lost that awareness. They feel their kinship with all who live. Some of the bond remains even with us, however, and may be seen in small ways—our instinctive love of songbirds, for example.

All is not sweetness and light in the non-human realm either, especially in this shaken and disturbed world. Rape has been observed among orangutans, dolphins, seals, bighorn sheep, wild horses, and some birds, although it is not the norm in any of these species.[9] But even in animal societies marked by male power, females generally remain self-sufficient and responsible for their own sustenance, unlike in most human (domesticated) societies. In some groupings, in fact, females provide for all. Lionesses do the hunting in their prides, for example.[10] Each elk herd is led by a cow, wise in the ways of coyote, wolf, lynx, cougar, and human. And it is also the case, according to many, that non-humans can be as individually distinct as we are. Delia Akeley concluded that "apes and monkeys vary in their dispositions as much as do human beings,"[11] and Barry Lopez commented on the "markedly different individual personalities" of wolves.[12] But one does see an absence of many old, infirm, and diseased animals among non-domesticates. How the "food chain" operates here brings up questions such as, do wolves only kill animals that are near their end anyway—the old, sick, injured? This seems to be roughly the case, according to Lopez.[13]

Hierarchy and dominance among other species is a long-running assumption, often a baseless one. The idea that there is usually, if not always, a "pecking order" derives from a Norwegian graduate student in 1922. His concept came from observing domestic chickens in his back yard and spread virulently in the animal studies field. It is a classic example of projecting from human domestication where, of course, hierarchy and dominance are indeed the rule. Its universality unravels with the fact that poultry yard pecking orders are not observed in wild flocks.

Similar is the fallacy that the Freudian paradigm of murderous rivalry between fathers and sons represents the state of nature. Questionable in the first application; even more so, evidently, regarding non-humans. Masson and McCarthy refer to zebra, kiwi, beaver, wolf, and mongoose fathers exhibiting acceptance and affection toward their offspring.[14] South American muriqui monkeys, female and male, are non-aggressive, tolerant and co-operative. Steve Kemper's "No Alpha Males Allowed" focuses on Karen Strier's work with the muriqui, which subverts the dominant view of male primates.[15] Among Asian gibbons, primates that live in pairs, the male may stay with his mate a very long time after sexual activity has ceased.[16]

John Muir described a goose attacking a hunter in support of a wounded companion: "Never before had I regarded wild geese as dangerous, or capable of such noble self-sacrificing devotion."[17] Geese mate monogamously and for life.

Widespread among non-humans are the social traits of parental care, co-operative foraging, and reciprocal kindness or mutual aid. Mary Midgley, in sum, referred to "their natural disposition to love and trust one another."[18] Also, to love and trust others, such as humans, to the point of raising them. Jacques Graven, in a striking finding, refers to children having been adopted by wolves, bears, gazelles, pigs, and sheep.[19]

In his irresistible *Desert Solitaire*, the cantankerous Edward Abbey imagines that the frogs he hears singing do so for various practical purposes, "but also out of spontaneous love and joy."[20] N.J. Berrill declared: "To be a bird is to be alive more intensely than any other living creature, man included…they live in a world that is always the present, and mostly full of joy."[21] To Joseph Wood Krutch it seemed that we have seen our capacity for joy atrophy. For animals, he decided, "joy seems to be more important and more accessible than it is to us."[22]

Various non-human intelligences seem lately to be much more highly regarded than in the past. John Hoptas and Kristine Samuelson's *Tokyo Waka*, a 2013 documentary film, looks at resourceful urban crows. How they use their beaks to shape twigs into hooks to snag grubs from trees, for example. In 2002, a New Caledonia crow named Betty was declared by an Oxford University researcher to have been the first animal to create a tool for a specific task without trial and error, something primates have evidently yet to achieve. Elephants' actions, according to J.H. Williams, are "always revealing an intelligence which finds impromptu solutions for difficulties."[23]

More surprising is what is coming to light about animals we usually consider to be further down the "food chain." Katherine Harmon Courage has uncovered heretofore unseen capacities of the octopus. "It can solve mazes, open jars, use tools. It even has what seems to be a sophisticated inner life." Courage goes on to state that the octopus "has a brain unlike that of almost any creature we might think of as intelligent."[24] Along these lines is a growing interest in "cold-blooded cognition," with recent studies revealing that reptile brains are not as undeveloped as we imagined. Lizards and tortoises, for instance, have exhibited impressive problem-solving capabilities.[25]

Jacques Graven was amazed to learn that the method of solving a maze is "scarcely different for a roach than for a rat," and that striking achievements by mammals "reappear in almost identical form in insects."[26] Speaking of mazes and the like, it may be added that very little of important truth is to be found in controlled laboratory experiments, whichever species may be subjected to them.

Memory is important to many creatures as an aid to survival. The work of animal scientist Tetsuro Matsuzawa demonstrates that chimpanzees have far stronger memories than humans.[27] Katydids have a hearing range many times that of ours. Honeybees can see ultraviolet light, invisible to us. The ichneumon fly can smell through solid wood. A monarch butterfly's sense of taste is two hundred times as sensitive as the human tongue. The dung beetle finds its way with reference to the Milky Way. Animals with four legs, and who don't wear shoes, probably pick up on a variety of emanations or vibrations lost on us. How about pet dogs or cats who are separated by hundreds of miles from their host families, and somehow find them? Only a kind of telepathy could account for the very many such cases.

A great deal more could be said about the gifts of animals. Or about their play. It is not "anthropomorphic" to recognize that animals play. Consider the mating dances of birds. I have seen the wonderful dawn dances of the sandhill crane. They dance, and have inspired an endless list of human societies. What of wild geese, whose matchless grace, elegance and devotion put us humans to shame?

Individuals of many species operate on an awareness that there is a distinction between "self" and "non-self." A member of one species can always recognize another of the same species. These kinds of self-recognition are obvious. Another instance is that of grizzly bears hiding out of sight of humans and others. There is a consciousness that the whole body—the "self" if you will—must be concealed.

But do non-humans realize that they are "selves"? Do they have self-awareness such that they realize their mortality? Many posit an absence of self-reflection and make this supposed absence the primary dividing line between humans and all other animals. Bees use signs, but are not conscious of their signing. On what basis, however, can we make assumptions about what bees or other animals know or do not know? Chimpanzees and orangutans recognize themselves in a mirror; gorillas cannot. What exactly does this reveal?

There is quite a set of unresolved questions, in fact, as to how conscious or unconscious human behavior is, especially in light of the fact that consciousness in ourselves is such a completely elusive thing. The complex, versatile, and adaptive responses we see as a rule among the living on this planet may or may not be guided by self-awareness. But self-awareness is not likely an all-or-nothing phenomenon. The differences between humans and others have not been established as radical; they are probably more a matter of degree. More fundamentally, we do not know how to even comprehend consciousnesses different from our own.

Our concept of self-awareness, vague though it is, seems to be the gold standard for evaluating non-humans. The other watershed condition is that of language: are we the only species that possess it? And these two benchmarks are commonly run together, in the assumption that consciousness can only be expressed by means of language. It is tempting to see in language the explanation for consciousness, to wonder whether the latter is only applicable to language-using beings. Indeed it can seem very difficult to think about the state of our minds without recourse to language. But if language were the only basis of a thinking order, all non-human animals would live in a completely disordered world, after all.

Wolves, dogs, dolphins, elephants, whales, to name a few, can vocalize at about the range of human registry. Humpback whale "songs" are complex intra-species forms of cultural expression across vast distances. It may be that animals' calls are, overall, more a matter of doing than of meaning.

If we look for our kind of symbolic meaning, it does not seem to be sustained among our fellow animals. In their natural state, parrots never imitate the human voice; species that may be seen to draw in captivity do not do so in the wild. Primates trained to master language do not use it like humans. Herbert Terrace, once a convinced ape-language researcher, became one of its harshest critics. Trying to wrest "a few tidbits of language from a chimpanzee [who is] trying to get rewards," says Terrace, produces nothing much of importance.[28]

Animals don't do what humans do via speech, namely, make a symbol stand in for the thing.[29] As Tim Ingold puts it, "they do not impose a conceptual grid on the flow of experience and hence do not encode that experience in symbolic forms."[30] An amazing richness of signaling, of the most varied kinds, does not equate to symbolizing. When a creature presents its intentional acts, it does so without the need to describe them, to re-present them.

The poet Richard Grossman found that truth is "the way it tells itself."[31] Jacques Lacan saw the orientation toward representation as a lack; the animal is without the lack that constitutes the human subject. At the heart of nature, wrote Joseph Wood Krutch, are the values "as yet uncaptured by language;" he added that the quality of cranes lies "beyond the need of words."[32]

I've long wondered how it is that so many animals look you in the eye. What do they mean by it? Gavin Maxwell enjoyed the "wondering inquisitiveness" of the eyes of Canadian porpoises,[33] while Dian Fossey's *Gorillas in the Mist* is filled with examples of gorillas and humans gazing on one another in trust. John Muir wrote of Stickeen, an Alaskan dog with whom Muir survived a life-threatening situation, "His strength of character lay in his eyes. They looked as old as the hills, and as young, and as wild."[34] John Lane was drawn by the eyes of alligators, an experience "not to be forgotten. Their black eyes hold steady as if staring through millions of miles or years."[35]

Maybe there's more to be learned there, in those direct windows, in that openness and immediacy, than by means of quite possibly unanswerable questions about consciousness and language. And if we could somehow see with those eyes, would it possibly allow us to really see ourselves?

There is an unmediated openness about the eyes. Death may be mentioned here, as perhaps the least mediated experience, or certainly among them. Loren Eiseley, near his own end, felt that wild things die "without question, without knowledge of mercy in the universe, knowing only themselves and their own pathway to the end."[36] Ernest Seton-Thompson's *Biography of a Grizzly* (1901) contains much about death. Today we are ever more distanced from encountering the reality of death—and animals. As our lives shrink, Thoreau's words from 1859 are all the more true: "It seems as if no man had ever died in America; for in order to die you must first have lived."[37] One need only add, it isn't humans who know how to die, but the animals.

As if in acknowledgment, humans have exacted a revenge on selected species. Domestication is a kind of death, forcing animal vitality into a subjugated state. When animals are colonized and appropriated, both domesticated and domesticators are qualitatively reduced. It is the proverbial "greatest mistake in human history" for all concerned. The direct victims, once quite able to take care of themselves, lose autonomy, freedom of movement, brain size, and what Krutch called the "heroic virtues."[38]

A farm pig is almost as much a human artifact as the farmer's tractor. Compare to a wild boar. Wild means free. To John Muir, wild sheep represented conditions before the Fall; conversely, he decided, "If a domestic sheep was any indication, Man's work had been degrading for himself and his charges."[39] The level of an animal's perfection, as Nietzsche saw it, was their "degree of wildness and their power to evade domestication."[40] In light of the vast picture of oppression, David Nibert calls the institution "domesecration," and it is not surprising that objections have been raised against even using the same name for wild and domestic members of a species.

Industrialism of course brought far worse lives on a mass scale, mass misery to feed mass society. Zoos and marine parks showcase further slavery, a fitting complement to the captivity at large. As the unbuilt, unmassified world recedes, the line between undomesticated and domesticated has blurred. Pretty much everything requires managing, up to and including the oxymoron "wildlife management." We are now in fact in a new age of domestication, including an unprecedented escalation of controlled animal breeding in recent decades.[41]

The completely non-biocentric, humanist myth of immortality is part of the ethos of domestication, its rituals focused on sacrifice rather than on the freedom of pre-domesticated life. Freud's Oedipal family model is a product of jointly domesticated animals and the father. Lacan's formulations often stem from findings about caged animals, and Kristeva's notion of abjection or disturbing threat, at base, refers to the act of domesticating. But the non-domesticated do not participate in assimilation into the conquered whole, in Freudian terms or otherwise.

Once there was a communal life of organisms in an ecosystem. Life fed on life, but not in a destructive trajectory. Even now we should not forget that the victory of domestication is far from total. Many species, for various reasons, are outside its orbit. "The lion tamer doesn't actually tame anything," John Harrington reminds us. He must stay within the boundaries the cats have established.[42]

"Almost everything about whales is a tantalizing mystery," concluded Diane Ackerman.[43] Wendell Berry quotes his daughter in his poem, "To the Unseeable Animal": "I hope there's an animal somewhere that nobody has ever seen. And I hope nobody ever sees it."[44] Do we need to know, can we know, so much about other animals? Maybe what we need most to know is that we could possibly join them in their non-domestication.

Kant was grievously wrong about human superiority. "As the single being on earth that possesses understanding, he is certainly titular lord of nature."[45] Walt Whitman provides a simple response: "Do not call the tortoise unworthy because she is not something else."[46] It is noteworthy that women dominate what is called animal ethology, and are far less prone to follow Kant's wrongheadedness.

The illusion of human domination of the natural world comes in many forms. One is the assumption that our prowess gives us long-range safety; we forget that this orientation can lead us into danger in the long run. Our lost connection, our lost awareness have led us into an age of horrors of every kind. And as Olaus Murie once said, "In the evolution of the human spirit, something much worse than hunger can happen to a people."[47]

Jacques Derrida came to see the prime importance of the question of animality for humans, as pivotal to "the essence and future of humanity."[48] The image of a free animal initiates a daydream, the starting point from which the dreamer departs. Meanwhile the living reality, the communion among species, yet manage to survive. The Inupiat Eskimo and Gwich'in people, who still travel without maps and discern direction without compasses, know that the caribou carry a piece of them in their hearts, while they carry the caribou in their hearts.[49]

The counsel of immediacy, of direct connection, has not been extinguished. "But ask now the beasts/ And they shall teach thee;/ And the fowls of the air/ And they shall teach thee;/ Or speak to the Earth/ And it shall teach thee." (Job 12: 7–8) In the Arctic Jonathan Waterman moved away from separation, from domestication: "I first removed my watch. My ability to isolate different and unidentifiable smells became incredibly distracting. My hearing seemed to improve."[50] Far from the Arctic, traces of this dimension have always been felt. Melville sensed in the sight of a sperm whale a colossal existence without which we are incomplete. One thinks of Virginia Woolf's use of animal vocabularies and inter-species relations.

Something whole, something unbroken, there millions of years before *Homo* showed up. Bequeathing to us what Henry Beston Sheahan called our "animal faith," which he saw being destroyed by the Machine Age.[51] We are lost, but other animals point to the right road. They are the right road.

We lack that state of grace, but we do know how much is in danger. Laurie Allman, taking in a Michigan songbird: "I can tell in a glance that he does not know he is endangered. He knows only that his job is to sing, this day, from the top of that young jack pine. His beak is open, full of the sky behind him."[52]

Here are Richard Grossman's lines in favor of a return to the old joy:

> **We shall forge**
> **a change of mind**
> **and come to understand**
> **the spirit as animal.**[53]

We are still animals on the planet, with all its original messages waiting in our being.

(ENDNOTES)

1   Quoted in Marc D. Hauser, *Wild Minds* (New York: Henry Holt and Company, 2000), p. 70.

2   Konrad Lorenz, *The Waning of Humaneness* (Boston: Little, Brown and Company, 1987), p. 70.

3   Aldo Leopold, *A Sand County Almanac* (New York: Ballantine Books, 1976), p. 83.

4   Henry Beston, *The Outermost House* (New York: St. Martin's Griffin, 2003), p. 25.

5   Jeffrey Moussaieff Masson and Susan McCarthy, *When Elephants Weep* (New York: Delacorte Press, 1995), p. 34. Among other works that indicate a shift away from anti-"anthropomorphism" are Ruth Rudner, *ask now the beasts* (New York: Marlowe & Company, 2006) and *How Forests Think* (Berkeley: University of California Press, 2013).

6   Eoin O'Carroll, "Oxford Junior Dictionary Dropping 'Nature' Words," *Christian Science Monitor*, February 9, 2009.

7   An ugly leftist counter-notion is communist Oxana Timofeeva, *History of Animals: An Essay on Negativity, Immanence and Freedom* (Maastricht: Jan van Eyck Academie, 2012), with Foreword by Slavoj Zizek. Timofeeva condemns nature's resistance to technology while bizarrely claiming that animals are natural communists! E.g. pp. 146–147.

8   Quoted in Susan Hanson, *Icons of Loss and Grace* (Lubbock: Texas Tech University Press, 2004), p. 182.

9   Masson and McCarthy, *op.cit.*, p. 140.

10 Barbara Noske, *Humans and Other Animals* (London: Pluto Press, 1989), p. 115.

11 Vera Norwood, *Made Fom This Earth* (Chapel Hill: The University of North Carolina Press, 1993), p. 235.

12 Barry Lopez, *Of Wolves and Men* (New York: Scribner Classics, 2004), p. 18.

13 *Ibid.*, p. 55.

14 Masson and McCarthy, *op.cit.*, p. 72.

15 Steve Kemp, "No Alpha Males Allowed," *Smithsonian*, September 2013, pp. 39–41.

16 Noske, *op.cit.*, p. 116.

17 John Muir, *The Story of My Boyhood and Youth* (Boston: Houghton Mifflin Company, 1912), p. 151.

18 Mary Midgley, *The Ethical Primate* (New York: Routledge, 1994), p. 131.

19 Jacques Graven, *Non-Human Thought* (New York: Stein and Day, 1967), p. 68.

20 Edward Abbey, *Desert Solitaire: A Season in the Wilderness* (New York: Ballantine Books, 1971), p. 157.

21 Quoted in Joseph Wood Krutch, *The Great Chain of Life* (Boston: Houghton Mifflin Company, 1956), p. 224.

22 *Ibid.*, p. 227.

23 J.H. Williams, *Elephant Bill* (London: Rupert Hart-Davis, 1950), p. 58.

24 Katherine Harmon Courage, "Alien Intelligence," *Wired*, October 2013, p. 84.

25 Emily Anthes, "Coldblooded Does Not Mean Stupid," *New York Times*, November 19, 2013, pp. D1, D5.

26 Graven, *op.cit.*, p. 127.

27 Justin McCurry, "Chimps Are Making Monkeys Out of Us," *The Observer*, September 28, 2013.

28 Quoted in Stephen Budiansky, *If a Lion Could Talk* (New York: Free Press, 1998), p. 45.

29 Kelly Oliver, *Animal Lessons: How They Teach Us to be Human* (New York: Columbia University Press, 2008), p. 186.

30 Tim Ingold, *Evolution and Social Life* (New York: Cambridge University Press, 1986), p. 311.

31 Richard Grossman, "The Truth," in *Animals* (Minneapolis: Zygote Press, 1983), p. 421.

32 Leopold, *op.cit.*, p. 102.

33 Gavin Maxwell, *Ring of Bright Water* (Boston: Nonpareil Books, 2011), p. 45

34 Edwin Way Teale, *The Wilderness World of John Muir* (Boston: Houghton Mifflin Company, 1954), p. 281.

35 John Lane, *Waist Deep in Black Water* (Athens: University of Georgia Press, 2002), p. 49.

36 Loren Eiseley, *The Night Country* (Lincoln: University of Nebraska Press, 1997), p. 173.

37 Henry David Thoreau, *The Journal, 1837–1861*, ed. Damion Searls (New York: New York Review of Books, 2009), p. 585 (entry for October 22, 1859).

38 Krutch, *op.cit.*, p. 102.

39 Michael P. Cohen, *The Pathless Way: John Muir and American Wilderness* (Madison: University of Wisconsin Press, 1984), pp. 173, 176.

40 Jennifer Ham, "Taming the Beast," in Jennifer Ham and Matthew Senior, eds., *Animal Acts* (New York: Routledge, 1997), p. 158.

41 Clive Roots, *Domestication* (Westport, CT: Greenwood Press, 2007), p. xii.

42 Quoted in Lane, *op.cit.*, p. 125.

43 Diane Ackerman, *The Moon by Whale Light* (New York: Random House, 1991), p. 112.

44 Wendell Berry, "To the Unseeable Animal," in Ann Fisher-Wirth and Laura-Gray Street, eds., *The Ecopoetry Anthology* (San Antonio, TX: Trinity University Press, 2013), p. 178.

45 Immanuel Kant, trans. J.C. Meredith, *Critique of Judgement* (Oxford: Oxford University Press, 1952), Part 2, Section 431.

46 Walt Whitman, *Leaves of Grass* (New York: Library of America, 2011), section 13.

47 Quoted in Jonathan Waterman, *Where Mountains Are Nameless* (New York: W.W. Norton, 2005), p. 237.

48 Quoted in Leonard Lawlor, *This is Not Sufficient* (New York: Columbia University Press, 2007), p. 7.

49 Waterman, *op.cit.*, p. 212.

50 *Ibid.*, p. 10.

51 John Nelson, "Henry Beston Sheahan," *Harvard Magazine*, September/October 2013, p. 40.

52 Laurie Allman, *Far From Tame* (Minneapolis: University of Minnesota Press, 1996), p. 73.

53 Grossman, *op.cit.*, "The New Art," p. 2.

Losing Consciousness

We might say that the three most momentous overall events have been the Big Bang, the emergence of life, and the arrival of consciousness. In terms of the third, everyone has a general notion as to what is meant. Very familiar—but elusive. In fact, consciousness has been called "the last surviving mystery."[1]

What exactly is consciousness? How does it come about? What does "consciousness" mean? Saying what constitutes jazz is a parallel slippery one. Hence the line, "If you gotta ask, you're never gonna know." The *Oxford Guide to Philosophy* puts it simply: "Consciousness exists, but it resists definition."[2]

It may be said to be perception of the inner environment or the immediacy of self-awareness. It is something so very central and yet, as Raymond Tallis asserts, most of what we do "can be carried out at least as well, and probably better"[3] without it. A pop culture fascination with zombies comes to mind, with at least one attendant question: with the frightening reality we face, is it any wonder that many would rather have less consciousness? In any case we certainly aren't zombies. Unlike them we seem to be mainly animated by ourselves, by a mysterious interior force.

Not forgetting the wound at the heart of present-day consciousness. The million or more young Japanese, for example, who suffer from what is called hikikimori, a kind of IT autism/withdrawal. The techno world is now our backdrop for any exploration of consciousness.

Nothing can be more real than our own consciousness, even if nothing is more difficult to spell out. It is so close to what it means to be alive. Thus it is hard to take seriously the claim of some neuroscientists that it is nothing more than the noise neurons make, an illusion. But Colin Tudge wonders how something that isn't conscious could somehow have illusions.[4] Thomas Nagel's "What Is It Like to Be a Bat?"[5] brings to mind consciousness as tied to our basic sense of ourselves.

Not only is there no accepted definition of our subject, "it is impossible," according to Stuart Sutherland in *The International Dictionary of Psychology*, "to specify what it is, what it does, or why it evolved. Nothing worth reading has been written about it."[6] In this vein, John Horgan noted that there are those who think that "consciousness might never be completely explained in conventional scientific terms—or in any terms, for that matter."[7]

Evidently what gives meaning to existence cannot supply meaning to itself. Without it nothing can be understood and yet consciousness remains an unanswered question, a profound and possibly eternal mystery. In terms of its emergence, for example, how could it speak to what was present in its absence, prior to consciousness? We know, after all, nothing but what consciousness puts there. It is impossible to reveal what it is by coming from the outside because there is no outside. The very effort to do so is something that is inside consciousness. As Ronald Chrisley put it, the difficulty is "not just that we don't have an objective understanding of this or that token instance of experience, but that we don't know how we could have an objective understanding of [that] experience at all."[8]

Freud was so very puzzled by consciousness that he turned almost entirely to the unconscious. It is also true, however, that in the field of philosophy of mind the literature on consciousness outstripped that on any other topic by two thousand. Locke said that consciousness is "the perception of what passes in a man's own Mind."[9] It is the realm of the knower being aware of their knowledge. But doesn't this beg the question? What exactly is such "perception" or "being aware"?

Consciousness may not be a single entity, but that which varies in kind as well as degree. Is it an entity? Brains are made of things, but is consciousness *made* of anything? It is not anything other than itself. It is unique and private, utterly first-person, and more than that. There seems to be a bedrock, bare-bones, nothing-but element or dimension somewhere in there, as well....

"Considered as to its specific nature, consciousness is a domain closed in itself, a domain into which nothing can enter and from which nothing can escape," wrote Aron Gurwitsch.[10] Sounds more like a black hole than our general sense of it. "No matter what theory we come up with," assayed Colin McGinn, "it always seems to run into some shattering difficulty."[11] Michael Frayn concluded, "Without it nothing can be understood; about it nothing can be said."[12]

We might look at a non-complex organism, one without a nervous system, as "conscious" insofar as it reacts, to, say, a change in temperature or a need for nutrients. But of course it is not self-conscious; it lacks a feeling of autonomy, among other things. For us, consciousness is the living nerve of the self, a mineness, what it feels like to be a particular kind of being. There is a unity of selfness capable of grasping oneself as oneself.

Consciousness of one's life is the background for all the other experiencing, while not forgetting the physical embodiment of it all. And a basic puzzle remains. Raymond Tallis noticed that "the harder the 'I' looks, the less there is to find that seems to be the 'I,' to be what the 'I' is."[13] What we are trying to comprehend is the me that is trying to comprehend it. The poet Anna Hampstead Branch cut to the chase: "What are we? I know not."[14]

Meanwhile, postmodernist thinking has done its best to deflate any claims to self-identity. Postmodernism marginalizes consciousness by asserting that it and the self are fundamentally no more than effects of language. The idea that language produces consciousness (cf. Emile Beneviste) is related to its corollary propositions, e.g. the denial of intentions and even of the presence of the speaker in speech (cf. Derrida), and the denial of the originality and coherence of the author.

Not only are these positions total surrender to the totalizing estrangement of the symbolic, they exhibit an ignorance of human development. Consciousness almost certainly preceded language by many thousands of years. We know that very significant human intellectual capacities are roughly a million years older than evidence of any symbolic ethos. And would not cognitive abilities necessarily predate language? How else could it be explained? Hence to claim that language causes consciousness puts the sequence plainly in the wrong order. There is also abundant case-by-case evidence that consciousness persists in individuals who have been deprived of language function.

Language does not create consciousness, and yet it is true that it is a hugely pervasive, confining presence. As Wittgenstein described, "A picture held us captive. And we could not get outside of it for it lay in our language and language seemed to repeat it to us repeatedly."[15] Robert Bly celebrates the captivity, missing Wittgenstein's point entirely: "I say, praise to the first man or woman who wrote down…joy clearly, for we cannot remain in love with what we cannot name."[16] The dependence on language is pointing at the moon and seeing instead the finger.

Laura Riding asked, "What were we, then, /Before the being of ourselves began?"[17] That beginning of consciousness seems to be much earlier than is commonly thought. As an artifact of human culture it necessarily arose in band society, our face-to-face hunter-gatherer mode of being for two million years or more, well over 95 percent of our tenure as a human species. It was assumed, moreover, that band society was based on kinship; that is, less a matter of conscious choice than the fact of being related to each other. Now there is strong evidence that this was not the case.[18] We were evidently self-aware selectors of our social and cultural attributes for much longer than was previously thought. In this vein, Paul Radin's work among Winnebago people showed him their reflective, individualistic qualities, which completely discredit the views of Tylor, Lévy-Bruhl, Cassirer, and others who viewed "primitives" as pre-conscious, pre-logical.[19]

Raymond Tallis saw "no evolutionary reason…why there should be consciousness at all."[20] Domestication of animals, plants, and ourselves in the bargain enters the picture about 10,000 years ago, and we might ponder its impact upon human consciousness. It is clear that non-human animals that are domesticated exhibit juvenilization or arrested development (cf. Lodewijk Bolk). Konrad Lorenz concluded in the 1960s that we also degenerate under domestication. There is a basis for what Roger Caras observed as our ambivalence about our own domesticated nature.[21] Cut off from a condition of intellectual freedom and unmediated connection to the natural world, ours is a place of lessened conscious range and acuity, almost certainly. Nietzsche frequently lamented the suppression of instinct, which is now even more evident in our increasingly deskilled and self-doubting existence. Now we find complete dependence on experts, and machines to replace the most basic conscious capacities.[22] Imagine: after so many thousands of generations we are now reaching the point where we need a machine to tell us what our infant needs. Domesticated consciousness moves forward, suppressing and eroding what we always knew.

William James held consciousness to be an awareness of the fleeting present, created and sustained by memory of the past and anticipation of the future.[23] That doesn't tell us, however, just what that awareness is or where it came from. It is also a formulation for a specific time and place; it relates to what Matthew Arnold called "this strange disease of modern life."[24] The "fleeting" present, the "anticipation" of the future are vivid for us, but they may have been missing altogether when the present did not flee before us and the future didn't need to be a matter of anticipation. Lacan's fatalistic ethic of the body comes to mind here. He describes a structure of anticipation in which the self is destined to fail,[25] fitting for an age of anxiety and foreboding.

In a context where experience is negative and threatening, consciousness is altered. Now it becomes useful to block out, not to open. Walter Benjamin referred to the role of consciousness vis-à-vis an often traumatic reality: "...the shock is thus cushioned, parried by our consciousness."[26] Benjamin's colleagues Adorno and Horkheimer saw that thinking has largely become "instrumental reason" under the deforming pressure of domination. Reason is no more neutral or privileged than technology—or consciousness. The instrumentality of the dominant order imparts a particular direction, at a basic level, to consciousness itself. In Foucault's view, subjectivity is invented and defined by the ascendant social institutions, to control us. Consciousness may be "a feeling about domain-specific capacities that have accumulated over millions of years of evolution," as Michael Gazzaniga put it.[27] It is also an artifact of that evolution, another marker of what has overtaken our species.

From Descartes to today, knowledge of the conscious subject seems to have taken on ever-increasing importance as the necessary first step in understanding. It is both the most intractable problem and the most philosophically resonant problem before us. It was central for Kant, though he erred in seeing consciousness as independent of any experience. Robert Brandom noted that "no Hegelian concept can be considered outside the economy of consciousness and self-consciousness."[28] In Hegel's idealist system, however, actual consciousness barely counted. Along these lines, Wilfred Sellars referred to him as "that great foe of immediacy."[29] Kierkegaard, the anti-Hegel, felt that Hegelianism made us forget what it means to be a conscious self.[30] But for Schopenhauer, awareness of our conscious self is torture; hence the goal is non-consciousness, an aim shared by Buddhists. Bergson was more positive. He defined consciousness as somehow a feeling of spontaneity.

Phenomenology (e.g. Husserl, Merleau-Ponty) celebrates the vitality and centrality of consciousness. Husserl described how the world is constituted through acts of consciousness, emphasizing the inseparability of perception and what is perceived, of consciousness from its objects. Intentionality is a key phenomenological term, meaning that consciousness is always active, always a consciousness of *something*. Another important phenomenological idea is that thinking must return to that which precedes it, to an originary, pre-conceptual presence or immediacy. This point is anathema to post-structuralist/postmodern types, who assail the notion that consciousness precedes the language used to describe it, and who mount an assault on the central role of consciousness in general.

Kenan Malik refers to a "bizarre love-in" between postmodernists and the neuroscientists who try to explain consciousness as a mechanism and hope to achieve its computer simulation. But he also understands that it isn't so bizarre that both camps "end up in this virtual world, because both abandoned the one thing that attaches all of us to reality—our conscious selves."[31] In a massively estranged world, it is also unsurprising that resistance to mechanistic approaches, even the most ghastly ones like transhumanism and cyborgism, is weakening. In fact, it is loudly asserted that the strengthening technological context of society is "rewiring" our consciousness to our detriment, at a basic level.

A relatively new entry is that of Roger Penrose, who proposes that quantum mechanics, in the person of neuron particles called "microtubules," may unlock the puzzle of consciousness. The logic seems to be that quantum physics is mysterious and consciousness is mysterious, therefore they must connect with each other.

Generally speaking, neuroscience looks at the mind as a complex computer or set of computational functions. The brain is of course the focus, and this organ is examined in minutest detail, but what is left out is what it feels like to possess a brain. A common assumption has been that computers would at some point become conscious, by becoming more complex and having greater capacity. But while we know why bigger mountains have snow and ice, we do not know why bigger brains have consciousness. Nothing that has emerged in computer technology (e.g. "Artificial Intelligence") is remotely like consciousness, no sentient device in sight. Neurophilosophy cannot give an account of consciousness that in any way corresponds to ourselves and our conscious lives. Returning full circle, as it were, how can we make a conscious machine work when we don't know what that would mean?

The nature of the relationship between the nervous system and consciousness remains murky and much debated. A dominant thread is that it has something to do with information processing. Some of our science heroes suggest that consciousness is indeed like information and that therefore we might be able to store it. On a very similar wavelength, they confuse machine computation with thinking and storage with memory. They forget that logical operations may be executed without consciousness—and seem to have nothing to do with it anyway!

Neural activity certainly bears on the shaping of consciousness and to some degree various processes of consciousness can be localized or located in the brain by cognitive neurobiology. The brain is obviously a necessary condition of any type of consciousness, not only self-consciousness, but nowhere is it shown to be a sufficient condition. Raymond Tallis is an invaluable resource on the topic and here is a deliciously pithy comment: "In so far as matter matters, the last word on its mattering lies with the consciousness to whom it matters."[32]

There is another point of agreement between postmodernists and neuroscientists (and a much larger number of people who are not aware of the assumptions and implications involved). This is the idea that consciousness is definitively representational. The postmodern tenet that there is nothing outside representation is intimate with the mechanistic identification of consciousness as symbolic processing, or representational. Postmodernists and neuroscientists share a pedigree going back at least as far as Socrates' belief that consciousness was pictures in the soul. But representation cannot precede self-awareness; it presupposes consciousness, as Tallis points out.[33] Is consciousness possible without representation? The weakness of the doubt thus expressed can be dispelled in various ways. For one thing, representation in the form of symbolic culture is a recent development among humans, dated by most archaeologists to the Upper Paleolithic. Thomas Wynn and others have deduced from archaeological evidence that humans were as intelligent as we are a million years before even the first symbolic artifacts, let alone symbolic cultures.[34] Is it at all likely, then, that they did not have consciousness?

It is more likely that representation diminishes consciousness. Other perspectives or dimensions are inhibited once the symbolic is established. Immediacy is lost. The injury thus initiated is a commonplace of philosophy, dating from Hegel if not earlier. And it is little wonder that a distrust or unease about symbolic culture and its hold over us is always somewhere present. Lacan referred to a primary lack at the root of consciousness, but the lack is representation itself. Nietzsche described consciousness as a "disease" among Europeans, coming close perhaps to naming culture as the cause.[35] Consciousness in the age of total representation has to be more damaged still.[36]

The idea that there are limits to our comprehension and that grasping our own consciousness may be beyond those limits is not a novel one. It seems to me that Colin McGinn has explained this very lucidly, in terms of representation. In sum: "While consciousness is a nonspatial phenomenon, human thought is fundamentally governed by spatial modes of representing the world."[37] I think McGinn captured the possibly insoluble heart of the challenge to comprehend consciousness. Like time, consciousness may not be subject to representation.[38] Echoing St. Augustine's meditations on time almost word for word, Sir William Hamilton wrote two centuries ago: "Consciousness cannot be defined; we may be ourselves fully aware of what consciousness is, but we cannot without confusion convey to others a definition of what we ourselves clearly apprehend."[39] Like time, consciousness may be nothing in itself, but there any resemblance ends. For the former, as an alienating, colonizing, dominating symbolic consciousness, is the bane of the latter. The inner reality of consciousness is active and fertile. We exert ourselves to plumb its full potential, to find what is preserved there, to find new states, a sharper self-presence, even if at times we also seek to be less than conscious.

Living under present conditions, our consciousness is haunted, and still we desire the open and undivided consciousness of the child, reminding us of what is almost a miracle, the polyphony of reality presented, not represented.

«

There is an often-told tale of a Pacific sailor who turns over his craft to islanders on an overcast, stormy night, and then marvels at their success at finding an island without so much as a compass.

When they arrived he asked, "How did you know that the island was there?"

The Native crew replied, "It has always been there."[40]

(ENDNOTES)

1   Daniel Dennett, *Consciousness Explained* (Boston: Little, Brown, 1991), p. 3.

2   Ted Honderlich, ed., *The Oxford Guide to Philosophy* (New York: Oxford University Press, 2005), p. 160.

3   Raymond Tallis, *On the Edge of Certainty: Philosophical Explorations* (New York: St. Martin's Press, 1999), p. 36.

4   Colin Tudge, review of Rupert Sheldrake's *The Science Delusion*, in *Resurgence*, August 2012, p. 61.

5   Thomas Nagel, "What Is It Like to be a Bat?" *Philosophical Review* LXXXIII (October 1974), pp. 435–450.

6   Norman Stuart Sutherland, *The International Dictionary of Psychology* (New York: Continuum, 1989), p. 90.

7   John Horgan, *The Undiscovered Mind* (New York: The Free Press, 1999), p. 247.

8   Ronald Chrisley, "A View from Anywhere," in Paavo Pylkkänen and Tere Vaden, eds., *Dimensions of Conscious Experience* (Philadelphia: J. Benjamins, 2001), p. 12.

9   Quoted in Barry Dainton, *The Phenomenal Self* (New York: Oxford University Press, 2008), p. 40.

10   Quoted in Richard Zaner, *The Context of Self* (Athens, Ohio: Ohio University Press, 1981), p. 89.

11   Colin McGinn, *Mind and Bodies: Philosophers and Their Ideas* (New York: Oxford University Press, 1997), p. 100.

12   Michael Frayn, *The Human Touch* (London: Faber and Faber, 2006), p. 401.

13   Raymond Tallis, *The Kingdom of Infinite Space* (New Haven: Yale University Press), p. 45.

14   Anna Hampstead Branch, "The Monk in the Kitchen," in Conrad Aiken, ed., *Twentieth-Century American Poetry* (New York: Modern Library, 1963), p. 42.

15   Quoted in Raymond Tallis, *The Explicit Animal: A Defense of Human Consciousness* (New York: St. Martin's Press, 1999), p. 88.

16   Robert Bly, "The Cry Going out Over Pastures," in *Selected Poems* (New York: Harper & Row, 1986), p. 140.

17   Laura (Riding) Jackson, "Nothing So Far," in *The Poems of Laura Riding* (New York: Persea Books, 1980), p. 318.

18   Kim Hill et al., "Co-Residence Patterns in Hunter-Gatherer Societies Show Unique Social Structure," *Science*, March 2011.

19   Paul Radin, *Primitive Man as Philosopher* (New York: Dover, 1957, especially pp. xviii, xxvi, 47, 231, 387.

20   Tallis, *op.cit.*, 1999, p. 188.

21   Roger Caras, *A Perfect Harmony: The Intertwining Lives of Animals and Humans Throughout History* (New York: Simon & Schuster, 1996), p. 160.

22   Domesticated life has reduced us intellectually and emotionally at a genetic level, argues Gerald R. Crabtree, "Our Fragile Intellect," *Trends in Genetics*, 13 November 2012.

23   Discussed in Stephen A. Tyler, *Mind, Meaning, and Culture* (New York: Academic Press, 1978), p. 138.

24   Matthew Arnold, "The Scholar Gypsy," in *The Poetical Works of Matthew Arnold* (New York: Oxford University Press, 1950), p. 195.

25   Vincent Crapanzo, *Imaginative Horizons* (Chicago: University of Chicago Press, 2004), p. 68.

26   Walter Benjamin, *Illuminations* (New York: Harcourt Brace, 1968), p. 162.

27   Michael S. Gazzaniga, "The Implication of Specialized Neuronal Circuits Versus Neuronal

Number for Concepts Concerning the Nature of Human Conscious Experience," in Gilbert Horman, ed., *Conceptions of the Human Mind* (New York: Lawrence Erlbaum Associates, 1993), p. 10.

28 Robert B. Brandom, *Tales of the Mighty Dead* (Cambridge, MA: Harvard University Press, 2002), p. 78.

29 Quoted in *ibid.*, p. 182.

30 Libus Lukas Miller, *The Individual in the Theology of Kierkegaard* (Philadelphia: Muhlenberg Press, 1962), p. 32.

31 Kenan Malik, *Man, Beast, and Zombie* (London: Weidenfeld & Nicolson, 2000), p. 352.

32 Tallis, *op.cit.* 1999, p. 55.

33 *Ibid.*, p. 121.

34 Especially Thomas Wynn, *The Evolution of Spatial Competence* (Urbana: University of Illinois Press, 1989).

35 Friedrich Nietzsche, *The Gay Science* (New York: Vintage Books, 1974), p. 300. 2012.

36 Lang Gore has considered lucid dreaming as evidently a gift of our earlier consciousness as humans and a possible future capacity. To navigate between conscious and unconscious zones is to be, he offers, outside representation and simultaneously creator, critic, and recipient. Who needed—or would need—art? Personal correspondence, July 1, 2012.

37 McGinn, *op.cit.*, p. 108.

38 My "Beginning of Time, End of Time," in *Elements of Refusal* (Seattle: Left Bank Books, 1988) discussed resistance to objectified time in similar terms. We seem to have tried to control or affect the growing materiality of time by spatializing or extending it in space, which only enlarged the problem.

39 Quote in Evan Squires, *Conscious Mind in the Physical World* (New York: Adam Hilger, 1990), p. 144.

40 David Lewis, *The Voyaging Stars: Secrets of the Pacific Island Navigators* (New York: W.W. Norton, 1978), p. 19.

The Sea

L ast remaining lair of unparalleled wildness. Too big to fail? The whole world is being objectified, but Melville reminds us of all that remains. "There you stand, lost in the infinite series of the sea."[1] What could be more tangible, more of a contrast with being lost in the digital world, where we feel we can never properly come to grips with anything.

Oceans are about time more than space, "as if there were a correlation between going deep and going back."[2] The Deep is solemn: linking, in some way, all that has come before. Last things and first things. "Heaven," by comparison, is thin and faintly unserious.

"Over All the Face of Earth Main Ocean Flowed," announced the poem by John Milton.[3] Given its 71 percent predominance on this planet, why is our world called Earth instead of Sea? Much of the land, in fact, could be defined as littoral areas where land and sea meet.[4] The sea is a textured place, infinite in its moods, forms, energies—and not so easily de-textured. But we see what happens when culture is privileged over place. The sea, where all life began just this side of four billion years ago, must still sustain us. Not only are its waters the original source of life, it also shapes the climate, weather, and temperature of the planet, and therefore the status of terrestrial species.

Kant saw truth as akin to an island surrounded by a stormy sea; water might "run wildly" and drown reason.[5] Chaos, disorder were always to be feared and brought under control. In Milton's paradise, the ocean is chafing under restraint,[6] suggesting that it can yield truth when freed. The power of nature is to be respected, not domesticated.

We come to life in water, in the amniotic fluid. Blood—and tears—are salty like the sea, menstrual cycles like the tides of the maternal sea, our mother. The sea is mountains rolling, sometimes calm and tempered. For Swinburne, "the storm sounds only/More notes of more delight...."[7] So many qualities, even phosphorescent at times, as I have seen on the Sea of Cortez. The seascape shows a magnificent array of fluctuating aspects and energies. John Ruskin found therein "to all human minds the best emblem of unwearied unconquerable power, the wild, various, fantastic, tameless unity of the sea."[8]

If the Earth is alive, the oceans are its most living parts. The sea whispers, croons, bellows in its unnumbered moods, always the "ground note of the planet's undersong," as George Sterling put it.[9] The very pulse of the sea, not only its perpetual motion, has us imagining that it is drawing breath. Inspirations and exhalations of a living, if unimaginably vast animal; many have written of the sea as a fellow creature. Malcolm Lowry recorded this meditation: "Each drop into the sea is like a life, I thought, each producing a circle in the ocean, or the medium of life itself, and widening into infinity."[10]

In the deep there is beauty and music; the sweeping surge of it is a matchless strength, a tireless spirit of freedom. Writing in his journal in 1952, Thomas Merton noted that every wave of the sea is free.[11] We might seek a heart like the sea: ever open and at liberty.

Loren Eiseley decided that "if there is magic on this planet, it is contained in water."[12] Why does running water, even a fountain or an aquarium, soothe or even heal? Far more potent, incomparable, is the spell of the ocean. "I was born in the breezes, and I had studied the sea as perhaps few men have studied it, neglecting all else," Joshua Slocum revealed in his late nineteenth-century account, *Sailing Alone Around the World*.[13] For many, the sea demands a deep loyalty, prompted by sheer wonder and the promise of peak experiences. A sense of being fully animal and fully alive. Ocean-hearted? The sea's staggering presence, its pure openness, brings on very powerful sensations. Rimbaud perhaps went furthest in trying to capture it in words:

> I have recovered it.
> What? Eternity.
> It is the sea
> Matched with the sun.[14]

As the young Joyce evoked the sea: "The clouds were drifting above him silently and silently the seatangle was drifting below him: and the grey warm air was still: and a wild new life was singing in his veins.... On and on and on he strode, far out over the sands, singing wildly to the sea, crying to greet the advent of the life that had cried to him."[15]

The sea, our deepest origin, calls to us. Sea-born, we are drawn seaward. Alain Corbin, discussing the work of Adolphe de Custine, recounts the latter's orientation toward that which "instinctively relates to our origins…." Namely, that the "sight of the open sea…contributes to the discovery of the deep inner self."[16] There is an exalting and revelatory experience possible in such a confrontation with the elements. We are humbled at the shore, on the waves, our presence a question. "The completeness and certainty of nature makes life bearable, less anguished," as Richard Nelson has written.[17]

When I was a small child at mid-century, our family sometimes drove west about sixty miles to visit my Dad's brother Ed on the central Oregon coast. My brother and I competed to be the first to see the ocean and cry "I see it!" It was a thrill to catch that first glimpse, every time. About thirty years later I came back to Oregon from California and worked in Newport at a shrimp cannery, near places called Boiler Bay and Devil's Punchbowl.

I don't think it's surprising that one can feel giddy at the massive sight. The Pacific encompasses fully one-third of the globe, sixty-four million square miles. Twice the size of the Atlantic. The absolute, (anti-)monumental There of it.

Is it not true that we are all somehow called to the sea by its lure, persuasion, gravity? Until he was forty John Ruskin was drawn to have "merely stared all day long at the tumbling and creaming strength of the sea."[18] A century later, Robert Frost wrote: "The people along the sand/All turn and look one way./They turn their back on the land./ They look at the sea all day."[19] Where every wave is different, and the heart and soul expand.

Loren Eiseley felt the Gulf of Mexico pulling him southward as he lazed in the Platte River. And more than that: "I *was* water…."[20] In 1826 Heinrich Heine had expressed a similar union: "I love the sea as my soul. Often, it even seems to me that the sea really is my soul."[21] Swimming in the ocean involves an "intimate immensity," to borrow a term from Gaston Bachelard. It connects with vastness and is inward, yet also a vigorous and robust experience. There can be challenges and perils, of course. Robert Louis Stevenson described a Hawai'ian woman who swam for nine hours "in a high sea," carrying the body of her husband home.[22] Albert Camus confided, "I have always felt I lived on the high seas, threatened, at the heart of a royal happiness."[23]

According to an article in the *American Historical Review* (2006), the maritime dimension has become a subject in its own right. "No longer outside time, the sea is being given a history, even as the history of the world is being retold from the perspective of the sea."[24] Unfortunately, its arrival on the stage has occurred on the heels and in the context of another inauguration, heralded by Gottfried Benn: "Now the series of great insoluble disasters itself is beginning."[25]

The fate of the once freshening sea is now that of crashing fish numbers, accelerated loss of marine and coastal habitats on a global scale, garbage gyres hundreds of miles across, dying coral reefs, growing dead zones (e.g. hypoxic zones in the northern Gulf of Mexico), to cite a few disastrous developments long in the making.

Water is "the most mythological of the elements," wrote Charles Kerenyi,[26] and the literature of the sea arguably began with Homer in the early Iron Age, eighth-century B.P. He wrote of its lonely austerity, "the sterile sea,"[27] a perspective that is certainly already that of civilization, poised against the natural world. The sea was by now merely a means, a passageway to increased domination, new conquests; large war fleets were well established. Aphrodite, goddess of love, arose from sea foam, but somehow failed to carry the day.

Seafaring is far older than history; it predates domestication/civilization by hundreds of thousands of years. Humans were navigating the oceans vastly earlier than we were riding horses, for instance. *Homo erectus*, about 800,000 years ago, crossed scores of miles of ocean to inhabit the island of Flores in the Indonesian archipelago.[28]

And even today, long voyages on the open sea are made by people with no use of metals. David Lewis marveled at a Pacific native who found his way "by means of a slight swell that probably had its origins thousands of miles away.... He had made a perfect landfall in the half-mile gap [between two islands], having navigated for between 45 and 48 miles without a single glimpse of the sky."[29] Thor Heyerdahl of *The Kon-Tiki Expedition* fame made use of the "Incas' simple and ingenious way of steering a raft" on his impressive South Pacific odyssey.[30] Interestingly, while the Incas revered the sea, the Mayas made scant mention of it—possibly because the Mayas had a written language and the Incas did not.

Joshua Slocum's account of his solo sail around the globe notes how the South Pacific islanders "take what nature has provided for them," and "have great reason to love their country and fear the white man's yoke, for once harnessed to the plow their life would no longer be a poem."[31] And his further South Pacific observation: "As I sailed further from the center of civilization I heard less and less of what would and what would not pay."[32]

Meanwhile, cannon-armed sailing ships had "heralded a fundamental advance in Europe's place in the world" in terms of control of oceanic trade routes.[33] In the late 1400s Portugal and Spain, the first global naval powers, competed for vast stretches of the Atlantic, Indian, and Pacific oceans. The worldwide commons of the seas was rather rapidly disenchanted and instrumentalized as the era of modern history dawned. Its relative solitude, silence, spiritual wealth, and intimacy gave way to the onslaught of globalization, and then industrial globalization.

The quiet gracefulness of sailing ships, and the seamanship skills of their crews, were ushered out in the nineteenth century in favor of graceless vessels, noisy and forced, like moving factories. How much globalized industrial existence is possible under simple sail? Voyages with time enough to know oceans and heavens, taking what wind and wave have to offer. Adventures, not timetables and technological disasters.

A sentiment opposed to the Machine was the sea as archetype and key source of the sublime in the Romantic era. The powerful sea paintings of Winslow Homer and J.M.W. Turner certainly come to mind. But celebrated or not, the oceans were being targeted for domestication. In *Childe Harold*, Byron wrote: "Man marks the earth with ruin—his control/Stops with the shore."[34] Later in the century his words no longer rang true. Joseph Conrad dated the end of the old sea from 1869, when the Suez Canal was completed.[35] In 1912 an iceberg quickly dispatched the largest moving object on the planet. *Titanic*'s demise was a blow to confidence in the complete mastery of nature, as well as the opening act of chronic contemporary disasters.

Peter Matthiessen's novel *Far Tortuga*[36] is a troubled meditation on the sea, with its background of a Caribbean region stripped of sea turtles, fish, timber, etc. by the 1970s. In fact, John Steinbeck described Japanese fishing dredges at work off the coast of Mexico in 1941, "literally scraping the bottom clean"[37] with a ravening, wasteful industrial process. The assault on the sea and its inhabitants is nothing new, but is always being intensified by advancing technology. An IBM SmartCloud ad of 2012 boasts of "smarter" computing systems that enable fishermen "to auction their catch while still at sea,"[38] to speed up the decimation of the oceans.

Long ago we had few things, on the water especially. Now we take our profusion of possessions with us. Mass society comes along on the voyage of industrial tourism. "Voyage" comes from *via*: away. But there is no more away. It is no coincidence that the survival struggles of indigenous peoples and aquatic life have reached a generally similar level of extremity.

"All the rivers run into the sea; yet the sea is not full." But Ecclesiastes 1:7 is no longer accurate. Rising sea levels, perceptible since 1930, are an alarming fact. "Other sea-cities have faltered,/ and striven with the tide,/ other sea-cities have struggled/ and died," observed H.D.[39] Trillions of tons of water are now a steady flow of polar ice cap melting.

Many studies and new books recount what is starkly clear. Rising temperatures, acidification levels and pollution; the North Sea has warmed to the point of tropical fish and birds in the fjords of Norway. The thermohaline circulation (vertical current movement) in the North Atlantic is weakening markedly.

Damaged, clearly, but not domesticated yet. A couple of lines from two anonymous poets: indicating the ocean, "Give me fields that no man plows/ The farm that pays no fee," and "The ocean's fields are fair and free,/ There are no rent days on the sea!"[40] To watch a fine surf for hours, to recall direct sensory experience—and ponder its severe diminution. Many have called the sea the finest university of life, free from the never-satisfied network of speech and the symbolic. Paul Valéry felt that "the quickening sea/ Gives back my soul…O salty potency!/ I'll run to the wave and from it be reborn!"[41]

There is a kind of purification motif that many writers have touched on vis-à-vis the sea. Rimbaud, for example, referred to the sea "which I loved as though it should cleanse me of a stain."[42] Jack Kerouac's first novel mentions "the way this Protean ocean extended its cleansing forces up, down, and in a cyclorama to all directions."[43] The once-scrubbed seas, soaking up the crime of civilization. John Steinbeck saw that "a breakwater is usually a dirty place, as though tampering with the shoreline is obscene and impractical to the cleansing action of the sea."[44] For Heyerdahl, the Pacific "had washed and cleansed both body and soul,"[45] echoing Euripedes' words: "The sea washes away and cleanses every human stain."[46]

Its own denizens show us so very much. The porpoises, that always prefer sailboats; the singing humpback whales; dolphins, with their extraordinary brain size and intelligence. Did not whales and dolphins return to the oceans, having found land life unsatisfactory? There is some kind of open telepathic connection among all dolphins in the sea, according to Wade Doak.[47]

"I will go back to the great sweet mother,/ Mother and love of men, the sea," wrote Swinburne.[48] The sea has many voices. "Deep calleth unto deep," to quote Psalms 52:7. All of life is connected, and the "oceanic feeling" aptly expresses a sense of deep bonds, a oneness. Not accidentally is "oceanic" the term employed to denote a profound connectedness. Robinson Jeffers told us that "mere use," meaning the technological, the fabricated world, "won't cover up the glory."[49] The glory of the sea, the glory of the non-fabricated world. He celebrated the wholeness of life and the universe, counseling "Love that, not man/ Apart from that."[50] Also remember, from the "French May" of 1968, "Sous les pavés, la plage."

On his Inca-inspired raft, Thor Heyerdahl discovered a deep truth. "Whether it was 1947 B.C. or A.D. suddenly became of no significance. We lived, and that we felt with alert intensity. We realized that life had been full for men before the technical age also—indeed, fuller and richer in many ways than the life of modern man."[51]

And we still have the sea, just possibly too big to fail. "Cease not your moaning you fierce old mother," wrote Walt Whitman,[52] whose truest poetry so often evoked the sea. Let's join with Byron: "Roll on, thou deep and dark blue Ocean—roll!"[53]

(ENDNOTES)

1 Herman Melville, *Moby Dick, or The Whale* (New York: Random House, 1930), p. 223.

2 James Hamilton Patterson, *The Great Deep: The Sea and Its Thresholds* (New York: Random House, 1992), p. 92.

3 John Milton, "Over all the Face of Earth Main Ocean Flowed," in *The Eternal Sea: An Anthology of Sea Poetry*, W.M. Williamson, ed. (New York: Coward McCann, 1946), p. 187.

4 Paul Rainbird, *The Archaeology of Islands* (New York: Cambridge University Press, 2007), p. 48.

5 Immanuel Kant, *Critique of Pure Reason* (New York: Cambridge University Press, 1998), p. 665.

6 "Under yon boiling ocean, wrapped in chains," for instance. John Milton, *Paradise Lost*, Second Edition, ed. Scott Elledge (New York: W.W. Norton, 1993), Book II, p. 38.

7 Algernon Charles Swinburne, "To a Seamew," in Williamson, *op.cit.*, pp. 276–277.

8 John Ruskin, *The Works of John Ruskin*, vol. 3 (London: George Allen, 1903), p. 494.

9 George Sterling, "Sonnets on the Sea's Voice," in Williamson, op.cit., pp. 510–511.

10 Malcolm Lowry, *The Voyage That Never Ends: fictions, poems, fragments, letters*, Michael Hof-

mann, ed. (New York: New York Review of Books, 2007), p. 239.

11 Thomas Merton, *Entering the Silence* (San Francisco: Harper, 1996), pp. 474–475.

12 Loren Eiseley, *The Immense Journey* (New York: Vintage Books, 1959), p. 15.

13 Joshua Slocum, *Sailing Alone Around the World* (New York: Sheridan House, 1954), p. 4.

14 Arthur Rimbaud, "Eternity," translated by Francis Golffing, in *The Anchor Anthology of French Poetry From Nerval to Valéry in English Translation*, ed. Angel Flores (New York: Anchor Books, 2000), p. 120.

15 James Joyce, *A Portrait of the Artist as a Young Man* (New York: Oxford University Press, 2000), p. 144.

16 Adolphe de Custine, cited in Alain Corbin, *The Lure of the Sea: The Discovery of the Seaside in the Western World*, translated by Jocelyn Phelps (Malden, MA: Polity Press, 1994), p. 170.

17 Richard K. Nelson, *The Island Within* (San Francisco: North Point Press, 1989), p. 129.

18 John Ruskin, *Praeterita* (Boston: Dana Estes & Co., 1885), p. 68.

19 Robert Frost, "Neither Out Far Nor in Deep," *Complete Poems of Robert Frost* (New York: Holt, Rinehart and Winston, 1964), p. 394.

20 Eiseley, *op.cit.,* p. 19.

21 Heinrich Heine, cited in Corbin, *op.cit.,* p. 168.

22 Robert Louis Stevenson, *Island Landfalls: Selections from the South Seas* (Edinburgh: Cannongate, 1987), p. 69.

23 Albert Camus, "The Sea Close By," *Lyrical and Critical Essays*, ed. Philip Thody, translated by Ellen Conroy Kennedy (New York: Alfred A. Knopf, 1968), p. 181.

24 Karen Wigen, "Oceans of History," American Historical Review 111:3 (June 2006), p. 717.

25 Gottfried Benn, cited in Ulrich Beck, *World Global Society* (Malden, MA: Polity Press, 1999), p. 108.

26 Charles Kerenyi, cited in Gaston Bachelard, *The Poetics of Reverie*, translated by Daniel Russell (New York: Orion Press, 1969), p. 177.

27 Homer, cited in Jules Michelet, *La Mer*, translation by Alice Parman (Paris: Gallimard, 1983), pp. 269–270.

28 Morwood et al., 1999, cited in Rainbird, *op.cit.,* p. 65.

29 David Lewis, *The Voyaging Stars: Secrets of the Pacific Island Navigators* (New York: W.W. Norton, 1978), p. 14.

30 Thor Heyerdahl, *The Kon-Tiki Expedition* (London: George Allen & Unwin Ltd., 1950), p. 84.

31 Slocum, *op.cit.,* p. 158.

32 *Ibid.,* p. 157.

33 Jeremy Rifkin, *Biosphere Politics* (New York: Crown Publishers, 1991), p. 103.

34 George Gordon, Lord Byron, cited in W.H. Auden, *The Enchafèd Flood, or The Romantic Iconography of the Sea* (New York: Random House, 1950), p. 16.

35 Joseph Conrad, *An Outcast of the Islands* (Garden City, NY: Doubleday, Page, 1923), beginning of Chapter 2.

36 Peter Mattheissen, *Far Tortuga* (New York: Random House, 1975).

37 John Steinbeck, *The Log from the Sea of Cortez* (New York: Penguin Books, 1995), p. 204.

38 "Smarter business for a Smarter Planet: The cloud that's transforming an industry, one fish at a time." IBM, 2012.

39 H.D., "Other Sea-Cities," *H.D.: Collected Poems 1912–1941*, ed. Louis L. Martz (New York: New Directions, 1983), p. 359.

40 Anon., "We'll Go to Sea No More" and "The Fisher's Life," in Williamson, *op.cit.,* pp. 309, 310.

41 Paul Valéry, "The Cemetery by the Sea," in Flores, *op.cit.,* p. 276.

42   Arthur Rimbaud, "The Alchemy of Words," in Flores, *op.cit.*, pp 127–128.

43   Jack Kerouac, *The Sea is My Brother* (Boston: Da Capo Press, 2011), p. 206.

44   Steinbeck, *op.cit.*, p. 17.

45   Heyerdahl, *op.cit.*, p. 97.

46   Corbin, *op.cit.*, p. 67.

47   Wade Doak, *Dolphin Dolphin* (New York: Sheridan House, 1981).

48   Algernon Charles Swinburne, "The Return," in Williamson, *op.cit.*, p. 18.

49   Robinson Jeffers, "Fierce Music," *The Beginning and the End and Other Poems* (New York: Random House, 1963), p. 57.

50   Robinson Jeffers, "The Answer," *The Selected Poetry of Robinson Jeffers* (New York: Random House, 1938), pp 57, 594.

51   Heyerdahl, *op.cit.*, pp. 132.

52   Walt Whitman, "Sea-Drift," *Leaves of Grass* (New York: Modern Library, 1921), p. 205.

53   George Gordon, Lord Byron, "Childe Harold's Pilgrimage," Canto Fourth, *The Complete Poetical Works of Lord Byron* (Boston: Houghton Mifflin, 1905), p. 179.

What Does it Mean to be Healthy?

What does it mean to be healthy, when dis-ease is the fact of modern life? As we know, there's no separating body and spirit, and here the main emphasis will be on the spirit.

Paraphrasing Adorno, Fabian Freyenhagen offered this judgment: "In a wrong world, no one can be healthy, live well or even rightly."[1] But if, amid the ruins, a wrong world consigns us to living wrong lives, at least we can resist our social world in both private and public spheres, and thus live less wrongly. The great impediment, of course, is that we really only attend to the private sphere. Billions are spent on various flavors of self-empowerment rhetoric, and the failure of this effort could not be more evident. If any of it worked, there wouldn't be such a constant flood of "self-help" commodities and focus on supposed therapeutic expertise.

The wrong world. The world of accumulated suffering and trauma.[2] "The Age of School Shootings;"[3] rising rates of suicide,[4] autism,[5] and obesity; the extinction of community. Widespread anxiety[6] and a kind of overall PTSD condition—and all so generally unthought, unexamined.

A passivity and a sense of doom have settled on modern industrial society, as we lose our connection to each other and the world. I noticed in the early 1980s that Gary Trudeau's comic strip characters began to have dark bags under their eyes. Not too much later, today's fashion models' expressions are blank and/or sullen. Smiles are very rare. As Philip Larkin's poem "Afternoons" concludes:

> **Something is pushing them**
> **To the side of their own lives.**[7]

Zygmunt Bauman goes so far as to assert that "we have indeed become, at least for the time being, 'invalids watching from hospital windows'."[8] We can at least identify with Dalton Conley's query, "What has happened to leave so many of us dangling in uncertainty each morning as we rise from our beds…?"[9] Strength and health are not about staying where one is or regaining that stasis. If there could be a kind of psycho-analysis of today's culture, Adorno decided, it would "show the sickness proper to the time to consist precisely in normality."[10]

High-tech consumerism and the market feed on the unhappiness and withdrawal from life they generate. There is a fragmenting, assaultive, and numbing quality to contemporary developed societies that injures human interiority deeply. Norman Mailer saw cancer as a result of the wrong world internalized. The madness is imprisoned within, goes into the tissues and cells and causes a tension that results in a mad "revolt of the cells."[11] This formulation seems plausible to me. The aggregate of pollutants certainly bears on the case of cancer, but so, too, does the force of massive estrangement.

The prevailing and invasive madness is a culture of nihilism, with such features as depression,[12] distrust,[13] loneliness,[14] and fear.[15] A restless inner emptiness is characteristic, especially since the 1970s. The manipulation or control of emotional life is a goal everywhere advertised, but it is not working; it's clearly incapable of producing joy or health. Franz Kafka captured the image of the victim "caught in the trap the world has turned into," as Milan Kundera put it.[16] Graduates are still being told, echoing Shakespeare's Polonius, "to thine own self be true"; but who thinks this relates to the world we endure?

How can we "feel and engage rather than become numbed and dulled by how much we face," in Sarah Conn's words.[17] At the same time, judging from the rise in mass "random" shootings, there are more "walking time bombs" out there. Lipovesky and Charles (among others) note "a worrying trend towards a greater fragility and emotional instability" among individuals.[18]

The meaning of health, the recovery of the art of healing, is to learn from our suffering, to see its sources. Ward Churchill, asked why he doesn't speak about healing, replied that there's no healing unless we stop the wounding.[19]

In the *Journal of Affective Disorders*, Brandon Hidaka discussed "Depression as a Disease of Modernity," contrasting past human environments with modern living.[20] He saw present-day "overfed, malnourished, sedentary, sunlight-deficient, sleep-deprived, and socially isolated"[21] denizens of disenchanted, dysfunctional, domesticated mass society as inherently prone to ill health. A brief look at some features of its opposite, hunter-gatherer life, will throw this even more clearly into relief.

At one time, and for a very long time, we lived literally close to our mother Earth. Relatively recently, our beds—especially in the West—have risen, as have our tables. Just lately, with ever more sedentism, we learn that a lot of sitting on chairs can be fatal![22]

Roland Barthes referred to our divorce from the Earth in his "Civilization of the Rectangle" remarks, pointing out a kind of "pollution effected by the rectangle, which very rarely occurs in nature."[23] Land ownership, a function of domestication, is the firm basis of the separation of humans from the natural world. Landed property is the original enclosure of reproductive resources, the control of both land and women. Along these lines, the privatized domestic sphere is also the invention of domestic violence.[24]

There were choices thousands of generations earlier than these developments, based on an intelligence equal to ours. Paul Tacon is on good grounds to surmise that very early humans (e.g. *Homo erectus*) probably "questioned their position in the universe."[25] They were far more robust than we are, and recent scholarship has significantly raised estimates of their longevity. Research has also confirmed very early cooking with fire: the appearance of small molars at 1.9 million years ago is evidence of cooked food, compared with the large molars of other primates who spend much more time chewing.[26] And it may not be amiss to bring in Montaigne's sixteenth-century essay, *Of the Custom of Wearing Clothes*,[27] where he observes that people remain who wear none, "situated under much the same sky as ours [France's]. Montaigne found it unhealthy, our practice of being so mediated against the elements, when we "are naturally equipped with sufficient covering...."[28]

Capabilities such as attention span, literacy, and depth of thinking are aspects of health. Too bad they're being fast washed away by the all-encompassing momentum of technology. In March 2014 the Scholastic Aptitude Test for high schoolers was dumbed down, excising the once required essay portion and deleting words thought too difficult in today's tweet and text world. In the lower grades the teaching of handwriting is being discontinued. That skill and aesthetic is no longer wanted for a life spent at keyboards, staring at screens.

We are told that we're empowered by all the technology, that it puts us in charge, but in fact we're swept along by it. We are free-floating subjects, more and more "bereft of any psychological traits or sociocultural specificity," according to Joanne Garde-Hansen and Kristyn Gorton.[29] And we are increasingly reliant on technological prosthesis for companionship, entertainment, and so much else. Early on, Jean Baudrillard called this "the end of interiority and intimacy."[30]

Milan Kundera once described the terrible elusiveness of living in the present moment: "All the sadness of life lies in that fact," he judged.[31] How much does technology rob us of well-being by chasing us from the present, from being present in the moment? In fact, its accelerating movement into every sphere means that all experience is decreasingly real. Vital, first-hand experience is in full retreat. Human relations have been traded for relations via machines. A 2014 news story reported that traditional dances and proms at John Jay High School in Cross River, New York, ended in 2011.[32] They were discontinued because students overwhelmingly preferred going home to text and tweet rather than attend dances.[33] The digital dimension has become the destination for more of everything people do. Even as cyber culture becomes ever thinner and more homogeneous, distracted, and superficial. William Powers refers to "the rushed, careless quality of screen communication,"[34] and John David Ebert adds that "Facebook does not allow for the possibility of long conversations of *any* kind."[35]

Can there exist a healthy autonomy from this pervasive and invasive medium? Considering the entire ensemble, how much free choice is there, given what is now required of us on an everyday functional level? We are personally diminished by our progressive de-skilling, which reduces our autonomy further, while elevating our dependence on specialists of all kinds.

There is a profound dissonance between our inner nature and the always-intruding technological environment. A disembodied, synthetic life-world means that we live less vigorously. Nietzsche saw plenitude as the key to health. Where is real plenty in the virtual? To be healthy means to live richly, challenging ourselves, becoming strong by stretching ourselves past accepted norms.

And who would deny that health has to do with love? Which is a way of seeing the world, or not seeing it. Nothing grounds and supports us more than love. Whatever warmth we share is our small splendor. In "An Arundel Tomb," Philip Larkin concluded, "What will survive of us is love."[36]

We also know that health, at base, only really exists within a just and humane society. It is healthful to resist unprecedented alienation and unfreedom. The alternative is not a healthy one.

We settle for so little as disaster closes in. We pretend that what forecloses our flourishing, impinges on how we could be healthy, isn't somehow, oppressively, everywhere. What a howl—and more—could burst forth from the yawning want that constitutes our lives. Health!

(ENDNOTES)

1   Fabien Freyenhagen, *Adorno's Practical Philosophy: Living Life Less Wrongly* (New York: Cambridge University Press, 2013), p. 5.

2   When what is taken for granted can no longer be assumed to exist, a generalized, traumatic anxiety results. Jeffrey Kauffman, ed., *Loss of the Assumptive World: A Theory of Traumatic Loss* (New York: Brunner-Routledge, 2002).

3   Jack Healy, "The Age of School Shootings," *New York Times*, January 16, 2014.

4   David Brooks, "The Irony of Despair," *New York Times*, December 6, 2013. "Walter Benjamin said of modernity that it was born under the side of suicide," Zygmunt Bauman, *Postmodernism and its Discontents* (New York: New York University Press, 1997), p. 12.

5   Andy Fisher, *Radical Ecopsychology: Psychology in the Service of Life* (Albany: State University of New York Press, 2013). "The dramatic rise in autism spectrum disorders," p. 205.

6   Dennis Smith, *Zygmunt Bauman: Prophet of Postmodernity* (Malden, MA: Blackwell Publishers Inc., 1999). The current culture is "drenched with anxiety," p. 25.

7   Philip Larkin, "Afternoon," in *Collected Poems* (New York: The Noonday Press, 1989), p. 121.

8   Bauman, *op.cit.*, p. 156.

9   Dalton Conley, *Elsewhere, U.S.A.* (New York: Pantheon Books, 2009), p. 9.

10 Theodor Adorno, *Minima Moralia: Reflections from Damaged Life* (New York: Verso, 1974), Thesis 36, p. 58.

11 Norman Mailer, *An American Dream* (New York: The Dial Press, 1965), p. 13.

12 Lennard J. Davis, *The End of Normal* (Ann Arbor: The University of Michigan Press, 2013). "Depression rates rise each year rather than diminish," p. 53.

13 Connie Cass, "In God We Trust, Maybe, But Not in Each Other," Associated Press, November 30, 2013.

14 Ami Rokach, ed., *Loneliness Updated* (New York: Routledge, 2013).

15 Michael A. Weinstein, *Structure of Human Life: A Vitalist Ontology* (New York: New York University Press, 1979). "The overwhelming motive that grounds our practical life is the desire to ward off fear," p. 53.

16 Quoted in Ulrich Beck, *Ecological Enlightenment*, translated by Mark A. Ritter (Atlantic Highlands, NJ: Humanities Press, 1995), p. 88.

17 Quoted in Fisher, *op.cit.*, p. 15.

18 Gilles Lipovetsky with Sébastien Charles, *Hyper-Modern Times* (New York: Polity, 2005), p. 85.

19 Ward Churchill, public talk, Eugene, Oregon. June 18, 2000.

20 Brandon H. Hidaka, "Depression as a Disease of Modernity: Explanations for Increased Prevalence," *Journal of Affective Disorders* 140:3 (November 2012).

21 *Ibid.*, p. 205.

22 Alexandra Sifferlin, "Why Prolonged Sitting is Bad for Your Health," *TIME*, March 28, 2012. Many other studies and articles underlined this in 2012 and 2013.

23 Roland Barthes, *How to Live Together: Notes for a Lecture Course and Seminar at the Collège de France (1976–1977)* (New York: Columbia University Press, 2013), p. 114.

24 Victor Buchli, "Households and 'Home Cultures'" in Dan Hicks and Mary C. Beaudry, eds., *Material Culture Studies* (New York: Oxford University Press, 2010), p. 502.

25 Paul S.C. Taçon, "Identifying Ancient Religious Thought and Iconography," in Colin Renfrew and Iain Morley, eds., *Becoming Human: Innovation in Prehistoric Material and Spiritual Culture* (New York: Cambridge University Press, 2009), p. 70.

26 See my "The Way We Used to Be," in *Future Primitive Revisited* (Port Townsend, WA: Feral House, 2012), p. 113.

27 Organ, Nunn, et al., "Phylogenetic Shifts in Feeding Time during Evolution of Homo," *Proceedings of the National Academy of Science* 108: 35 (August 30, 2011).

28 Michel Eyquem de Montaigne, *The Complete Essays of Montaigne* (Stanford, CA: Stanford University Press, 1958), pp. 166-169.

29 *Ibid.*, p. 167.

30 Joanne Garde-Hansen and Kristyn Gorton: *Emotion Online: Theorizing Affect on the Internet* (New York: Palgrave Macmillan, 2013), p. 139.

31 Jean Baudrillard, "The Ecstasy of Communication," in Hal Foster, ed., *The Anti-Aesthetic* (Port Townsend, WA: Bay Press, 1983), p. 133.

32 Milan Kundera, *The Art of the Novel* (New York: Grove Press, 1988), p. 25.

33 Carolyn Moss, "My High School No Longer Holds Dances Because Students Would Rather Stay Home and Text Each Other," *Business Insider*, March 10, 2014.

34 William Powers, *Hamlet's Blackberry* (New York: HarperCollins, 2010), p. 53.

35 John David Ebert, *The New Media Invasion* (Jefferson, NC: McFarland & Company, 2011), p. 59.

36 Philip Larkin, *The Whitsun Weddings* (London: Faber and Faber, 1964), p. 46.

Why Hope?

t's pretty fashionable, among anarchists as well, to sneer at the notion of hope, to explicitly rule out any chance of overall victory over domination and oppression. *Desert* (2011) sports this outlook on its cover: "In our hearts we all know the world will not be 'saved'," and repeats this statement twice more in its opening pages. Civilization will persist. It's time to give up on "unwinnable battles." In this way the misery of burnout and disillusionment will be avoided and we'll all be a lot happier (!) The Mexican Unabomber-type group, Individualidades Teniendo a lo Salvaje (ITS), also firmly asserts that there'll be no winning. "We do not believe this is possible," they proclaim repeatedly.

But it is possible. Our overcoming the disease of civilization is in no way guaranteed, obviously, but clearly it is possible. I prefer what Kierkegaard said of hope: It is "the passion for the possible." More boldly, whatever became of "Demand the Impossible"? When victory is refused are we not at Game Over?

We might recall Herbert Marcuse's *One-Dimensional Man*, which announced the apparent end of radical possibilities, the definitive triumph of consumerist unfreedom. He was delighted to have been proven wrong within weeks of the book's 1964 appearance by the beginnings of a global movement that shook the world. And as the global system now shows itself to be failing at every level, shows itself to have no answers at all, there stands every chance of qualitatively surpassing the Movement of the '60s. But not, needless to say, if we renounce any hope of overcoming. It is well-known that health and recovery from illness is tied not to hopelessness but its opposite. Consider the Serbian Danilo Kis' last novel, *Psalm 44*, about a young family's will to survive and resist in Auschwitz, where visualizing hope is a "necessity." For us and all life, matters are grave but we are not in Auschwitz. And yet we spurn hope? Egoism and nihilism are evidently in vogue among anarchists and I'm hoping that those who so identify are not without hope. Illusions no, hope yes. I wonder what we have to offer at large, in terms of, say, analysis and inspiration – or whether that's still being asked much.

There are egoists who seem mainly in love with their sacred Egos, where all is judged insofar as it serves the Self. Meanwhile the reigning techno-culture feeds solipsism, narcissism, and isolation the more techno-addicted are its subjects. Did Max Stirner see the natural world as having value only in relation to one's ego? How much interest does the pure egoist have in mutual aid, social struggles or the disappearance of community? I recommend Stirner's *The Ego and its Own* as an important corrective to the appeals of collectivism in its various guises, but tend to agree with Arizona anarchist Dan Todd that Diogenes and the Cynics in the West and Chuang-Tzu and some of the Taoists in the East did an even better job of it centuries earlier.

Does nihilism mean that pretty much everything must go for a decent life to be possible? If so then I'm a nihilist. It's safe to say that nihil-ism isn't literally nothing-ism or one couldn't be both a nihilist and an anarchist. If it means the politics of desperation or hopelessness, no thanks. French philosopher Jean-Francois Lyotard put the word in a different light: "With the megalopolis, what the West realizes and diffuses is its nihilism. It is called development." Are there nihilists who take on such institutions and what drives them?

There's more than anti-hope on offer, in any case. Two new books remind us of that. Enrico Manicardi's *Free from Civilization* is the first 'A-Z' type anti-civ offering in any language (originally *Liberi dalla Civiltà*) and Paul Cedenec's *The Anarchist Revelation: Being What We're Meant to Be*, the least pessimistic book I can recall reading. It refers to German anarchist Gustav Landauer, for instance, for the idea that we "need not worry that the quantity of those answering the call will not be great enough, when the quality of its [anti-civ] content is beyond question." It brings anarchist resistance and the spirit together in a very wide-ranging and powerful contribution.

Dire times but, as Oscar Wilde had it, "We are all in the gutter but some of us are looking at the stars."